SECOND EDITION

SURVIVING INFIDELITY

Also by Dr. Gloria G. Harris

Assertive Training for Women (with Susan M. Osborn)
The Group Treatment of Human Problems

SECOND EDITION

SURVIVING INFIDELITY

Making Decisions, Recovering from the Pain

Rona Subotnik, M.F.C.C.
&
Gloria G. Harris, Ph.D.

Adams Media Corporation
Avon, Massachusetts

Published by
Adams Media Corporation
57 Littlefield Street, Avon, MA 02322. U.S.A.

ISBN: 1-58062-137-6

Printed in Canada

J I H G F E D

Library of Congress Cataloging-in-Publication Data
Subotnik, Rona.
Surviving infidelity : making decisions, recovering from the pain / Rona Subotnik & Gloria G. Harris. — 2nd ed.
p.   cm.
Includes bibliographic references (p.   ) and index.
ISBN 1-58062-137-6
1. Adultery. 2. Marriage. I. Harris, Gloria G. II. Title.
HQ806.S89   1999
306.73'6—dc21   98-52229
CIP

This book is available at quantity discounts for bulk purchases.
For information, call 1-800-872-5627.

Visit our home page at http://www.adamsmedia.com

To my husband, Norman, whose support and encouragement make dreams possible.

— R.B.S.

To my husband, Jay, for his love and devotion.

— G.G.H.

Contents

Part I
Understanding Infidelity

Part II
Coping and Healing

Part III
Dealing with the Marital Crisis

Part IV
Surviving

Appendixes

Preface

Surviving Infidelity is a book for women and men whose lives have been disrupted by infidelity. We have written this book to help our readers cope with extramarital involvement, to learn more about its dynamics, and to understand the accompanying web of feelings, thoughts, and actions. For thousands of years and continuing to the present, the marriage contracts of Judeo-Christian cultures have prohibited extramarital sex. Whether two people commit to each other through marital vows or by solemn promises, sex with another person causes emotional pain to the betrayed and harms the relationship.

Because infidelity can be devastating to marriage, it is important to resolve the crisis and rebuild the relationship whenever possible. The first choice for accomplishing this is to work with a therapist. However, for many couples, this is not always an option, for a variety of reasons. Sometimes finances or embarrassment may prevent them from finding help. Often the unfaithful partner does not want to come for counseling. This book has been written to help those individuals who may be trying to work out their problems without professional help.

Much of what we discuss in *Surviving Infidelity* has been drawn from our combined clinical experience as psychotherapists. In the safety of the therapy session, we have heard about pain and seen the disruption to families caused by infidelity. Because extramarital sex still plays a role in the dissolution of many marriages, and because the divorce rate continues to be high, it is important to know more about it.

In most cases our goal is to keep the marriage together. We view infidelity from a family perspective that takes into account the complexity of each person's past and current history as well as the social context. Our hope is to help you heal the wounds of infidelity and to strengthen the relationship.

Rona Subotnik is a marriage, family, and child counselor. Gloria Harris is a clinical psychologist. Together we have witnessed the impact of infidelity on the lives of hundreds of women and men whom we have counseled, both individually and in groups. When cases have been used, we have disguised the identities of our clients.

Let us begin with some definitions. *Adultery* is a legal term defined as *sexual relations with someone other than one's spouse. Infidelity* literally means *unfaithfulness* or *disloyalty*. It is the breaking of a promise or vow. An *affair* is defined as *an illicit amorous relationship or liaison*. We all have heard expressions like *messing around, fooling around, wandering, straying*, and *a little on the side*. Because they are used lightly, these expressions tend to minimize or ignore the seriousness of the infidelity and camouflage the emotional pain it causes.

Cheating, another commonly used term, is defined as *depriving someone of something expected*. Because the spouse is unaware of the infidelity, the couple is deprived of sharing experiences and building memories together. This creates a relationship based on deceit and dishonesty.

The first part of this book is called "Understanding Infidelity." In it we explore the various types of affairs and the reasons why they are likely to happen. It is important for you to know that not all affairs are the same. We have presented five basic types of affairs, which fall along a continuum according to the offending spouse's degree of emotional investment in the third party. Understanding what type of extramarital involvement is involved will tell you how serious it is. Knowing the reasons why affairs occur will give you information about causes and help you resolve the crisis in your marriage. Unfaithful spouses lie about affairs for a variety of reasons. In this updated edition, we have added new material on the impact on your marriage of revealing the truth.

The second part of the book, "Coping and Healing," provides you with some important skills for dealing with the blow. We present a cognitive approach based on the principle that by changing the way you interpret and view your situation, you can influence the way you feel, make wiser decisions, and act more productively. Over the past decades, cognitive therapy has become one of the fastest-growing and most effective approaches to treating human problems. In this part of the book we will aid you in your grief work and present ways to cope with your pain, rage, and jealousy.

In the third part of the book, "Resolving The Marital Crisis," we help you and your partner repair your relationship and aid you in letting go of hurt and resentment. We try to make it possible for you eventually to put your spouse's infidelity behind you and develop a stronger relationship.

There are also other alternatives. In some marriages the betrayed partner will choose to tolerate the infidelity. For others, separation or divorce will be selected as the most desirable option. We will present factors for you to consider as you make your decision either to continue or to end your marriage.

If the decision is to stay, we assist you in strengthening and revitalizing the post-affair marriage. Included are the ingredients of a successful marriage based on rebuilding trust, improving communication, and forgiving your spouse.

In the last part of the book, "Surviving," we teach coping skills and strategies. For those whose marriage is ending by choice of either spouse, we will present our ideas for dealing effectively with your new status and accompanying concerns. We present strategies for handling loneliness, making a new beginning, and developing more rewarding relationships. Because infidelity significantly affects your self-esteem, we have included a chapter discussing its roots. This chapter contains exercises designed to enhance the way you feel about yourself. The book ends with the chapter entitled, "What It Takes To Be A Survivor," which is intended to empower and inspire you. Whatever your decision, surviving infidelity ultimately involves facing new challenges.

It is customary to wish people good luck when embarking on a journey. We wish you good luck and good skill in turning a crisis in marriage into an opportunity for growth.

Acknowledgments

We wish to thank Norman Subotnik for his invaluable help, suggestions, and support. Our appreciation goes to the many members of the Subotnik and Harris families for reading the text and sharing their impressions with us. We especially appreciate the support in the Subotnik clan of Norman, Debra and Matthew, Kenneth and Stephanie, Adrienne and Todd; and in the Harris family, of Jay, Cameron, and Merrill. Thanks also to our friend Fran Zimmerman for her helpful suggestions.

Our very special thanks to our editors, Edward Walters and Brandon Toropov, for their highly professional guidance and capable assistance along our literary journey.

Rona Subotnik wishes to thank the wonderful women in Rockville, Maryland who make up the heart and soul of A Woman's Place (now known as The Commission For Women Counseling and Career Center), and the Montgomery County Government Commission for Women, for their support and encouragement when she was a staff counselor, for the amazing way that relationship has continued over a distance of three thousand miles since she moved to San Diego, and for the efforts they make every day to improve the lives of the women of Montgomery County.

It was there, as a counselor, that she first began to hear stories of infidelity from the brave women coping with its aftermath. Special thanks also to Wendy Plotkin-Mates who with Rona Subotnik led support and counseling groups for seven years, often as many as four a week. One of these groups was called Surviving Infidelity.

A final note of acknowledgment and appreciation goes to the women and men who have shared their stories with us throughout the years and whose courage inspired us to write this book.

— *Rona B. Subotnik & Gloria G. Harris*

Part I

Understanding
Infidelity

Chapter 1

All Affairs Are Not the Same

"Frankie and Johnny were lovers,
my God how they could love,
Swore to be true to each other,
just as true as the stars above.
He was her man, but he done her wrong."
— *FRANKIE AND JOHNNY*, TRADITIONAL

"I remember this enormous commotion in my neighborhood when I was a little girl," Janet reminisced in our support group. "I was playing paper dolls with Carolyn Ryan when her father ran outside yelling. Carolyn started to cry. We were both very scared. None of the adults would tell us what was happening, but later the older kids said Mr. Ryan came home early and found his wife in bed with another man.

"It was quite a neighborhood scandal," Janet continued. "Nobody on our block had ever done such a thing. I know, that was forty-five years ago, but still, why is there such a change? Four spouses on our little cul-de-sac of eight homes have had affairs, and that includes my husband Richard."

Janet is correct. Social attitudes have changed dramatically in the last forty-five years, and these changes have affected family life and marriage in profound ways.

Studies of affairs report considerable variations in their frequency. Some say that 60 percent of men and 40 percent of women have affairs, but other studies indicate lower figures, like 37 percent for men and 29 percent for women. Moreover, other reports claim that in couples therapy a total of 55 percent of the couples deal with infidelity issues, either when initiating or at some point during therapy. Our own clinical observations confirm that the chance that a marriage will be touched by infidelity is high, and that extramarital sex still plays a role in the dissolution of many marriages.

Infidelity, whether resulting in divorce or reconciliation, has a ripple effect that reaches far from the center and disturbs the security, peace of mind, and self-esteem of all family members. We would like to help you get a little distance from your emotional reactivity so that you can understand what may have happened and make the choice that will bring equilibrium to your life and allow you to move forward. Let's begin by examining how affairs differ.

Types of Affairs

"I just don't know how serious it is," Joyce explained to the support group as she told them about her husband Joel's affair with a woman in his office. "He says it means nothing, just a one-time thing. And he promised never to see her again."

"Don't believe him," replied Don. "I believed my wife, and now she's head over heels in love with the other guy, and we're getting a divorce!"

Are Joyce and Don in different situations? They seem to be. Joyce's husband and Don's wife have different depths of feelings about their affairs. All affairs are not the same, and the differences are very important.

The question Joyce raised in the group about the seriousness of her husband's affair can be answered when we know what type of affair it is.

From our work with men and women, we believe that affairs fall along a continuum according to the degree of emotional investment the unfaithful spouse feels toward the lover. At the beginning of the continuum are the casual involvements, like serial affairs and flings, in which there is no emotional connectedness. Further along the continuum are romantic love affairs with a high degree of emotional investment, and at the extreme end are long-term affairs, which last for years—possibly over the lifetime of the marriage.

The following diagram describes this continuum:

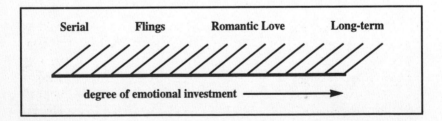

| Serial | Flings | Romantic Love | Long-term |

degree of emotional investment ⟶

Affairs

Although most of the infidelity we have seen is concentrated in these four areas, as in any continuum there may be movement. An affair can change in the degree of emotional investment. For example, what starts as a meaningless fling can change to a romantic love affair, and romantic love affairs can grow into long-term attachments. Knowing where the affair falls on the continuum helps you answer one of the core questions, which is, "Where does the commitment of the unfaithful partner lie?"

Serial Affairs

Let's start with a look at the affair in which the partners lack emotional investment: the serial affair. This can be a series of one-night stands and/or a series of many affairs. Having many affairs and partners indicates a wish to avoid involvement or intimacy, not a desire for emotional closeness. The relationship is for the excitement of the "here and now." Intimacy and commitment are missing in the serial affair. The lure in such cases is for sex and excitement.

Even though this is a sexual relationship, we see it as a way to "distance." In this category, regardless of gender, are the lovers we've come to call Don Juans and Casanovas. They often rationalize their behavior by thinking that they love and provide for their mates, but "a little on the side" doesn't hurt anyone.

Partners who have serial one-night stands are content to leave it at that. Meeting again would produce anxiety and complicate their lives. Many such affairs occur out of town, safely away from family and friends who may encounter them accidentally. Some occur at conferences or while traveling.

We have heard many stories from clients whose partners are repeatedly unfaithful. As Susan, a forty-three-year-old mother of three told us about her husband Ted, "He's screwing around with those damn women on his trips. His boss is, too. They're all doing it, and protecting each other. I know it, because I hired a private investigator. I'm so angry. I don't know what to do.

"When we got married, we struggled and worked together building what I thought was 'the good life.' With Ted's abilities and his dad's connections he landed a job in a local bank. He was so good that before long he was made a manager and eventually a vice-president," she explained.

"Our dreams of success were beginning to come true. Only it turned out to be a nightmare," she cried. "I had no idea what Ted was doing. He must have been laughing up his sleeve. He was away from home a lot, traveling to branches in other cities and going to these high-level meetings. Well, Mr. Rhinegold, the private investigator, told me that Ted and his colleagues began to have 'escorts,' young women who provide them with sex for a price. 'It doesn't mean anything,' Mr. Rhinegold said, 'It's a different one every time,' he told me."

Susan went on angrily, "Well, I don't give a damn what Mr. Rhinegold said. I am furious that Ted has 'escorts' and a secret life apart from me and the kids. I want it to end. I hate him for it." To Susan, Mr. Rhinegold's observation that "it's a different one every time" was the good news and the bad news. The good news was that the women never meant anything to Ted, but the bad news was that he had quite a history of infidelity. Ted was a serial lover.

Although Ted had many one-night stands, some serial lovers have a series of brief affairs. Our observations show the affairs usually last a few months but can last more than a year. We place serial affairs at the beginning of the continuum because there are no plans to make or maintain a commitment to the lover. A pattern often emerges for how the couple deals with the infidelity, if discovered. The partner is contrite, remorseful, and more attentive. He (or she) asks for forgiveness and promises not to be unfaithful again. He may start out with good intentions to be the faithful spouse, but in time the same pattern recurs with a new partner. After a few of these affairs, the offended spouse begins to recognize the signs and is aware that once again the marriage partner is unfaithful.

Many of our clients who are married to serial lovers come to recognize that the behavior will not stop, that their partners are addicted to sex. These spouses seem powerless to control their desire for sex. It satisfies their need for the excitement of the moment, even though it frequently creates problems and embarrassments in other aspects of their lives.

Men who engage in this serial kind of affair are often labeled "womanizers." A well-known example of this type is former Senator Gary Hart, who had much to lose from his behavior, since, at the time he was seeing another woman, he was a contender for the Democratic nomination for president. Indeed, his activities, under intense scrutiny by the press, were made public, ending his political aspirations.

In the past, the peccadilloes of Presidents John F. Kennedy and Lyndon Johnson had been kept secret during their terms of office. Although reporters were aware of them, they did not disclose the infidelities to the public on the grounds that such behavior did not adversely affect their performances as president. At the time, it seemed that the public's rejection of Gary Hart clearly indicated disapproval of infidelity by the American public.

That conclusion was reinforced in 1998, when the public learned the details of President Clinton's affair with a twenty-one-year-old White House intern, Monica Lewinsky. Polls taken three days after Kenneth Starr, the independent counsel, submitted his report to the House of

Representatives showed that a significant number of people disapproved of the President's infidelity. These polls did not show that the public wanted Mr. Clinton to resign his office or be impeached. However, many people felt his conduct should not go unpunished. Even when all the sexual encounters were so graphically detailed in the report, Mr. Clinton's approval rating remained extremely high at 68 percent.

One conclusion that can be drawn from these polls is that even though the American public is sophisticated enough to separate personal behavior from job performance, it still values fidelity in marriage.

If you are married to a serial lover, you may already know, or you may have been relieved to hear, that your partner has no significant emotional investment in these affairs. However, as you probably expect, there is a serious aspect to this kind of infidelity. Although there is no commitment to the sexual partner, there is also none to the marriage vow of fidelity. In this kind of infidelity, the affair is not serious, but the unfaithful behavior is.

Even though serial affairs fall very low on the continuum of emotional investment, they are significant because such infidelities usually continue for a long period over the course of the marriage. Although such behavior is not impossible to stop, it is unlikely to. Many such affairs occur with sexually addicted partners or with individuals who have histories of stormy relationships and self-centered behavior. If the behavior does end, it is most likely because of some dramatic happening, like a death in the family, a serious illness, or a loss of power and position.

One client, Jerry, told us he finally stopped "fooling around." It took a heart attack to do it. "Sure, I was stupid, but I'm going to try to make my marriage work."

Another case of reversing long-term infidelity was told by author Peggy Vaughn. In her book *The Monogamy Myth*, she relates her personal story of anguish about her husband's infidelities over a period of seven years and his complete turnabout to become monogamous. She attributes this to a combination of her own growth, her honesty, and her willingness to discuss the affairs in a nonjudgmental way. She concludes that even infidelity that has continued for many years can be ended. Peggy and her husband, James, a psychologist, have gone on to help thousands of people survive infidelity through their workshops and books.

When such behavior occurs, couples have much work to do to heal the wounds that develop from years of deceit. Building trust is a slow process when it has eroded over a long period of time.

Serial lovers have always posed a threat to the spouse because of the possibility of contracting a sexually transmitted disease. Today, the specter of AIDS makes that possibility a deadly one. We will have more to say about this when we discuss decision-making.

Flings

Next on the continuum is the fling, a kind of infidelity that, like the serial affair, is characterized by a lack of emotional investment. The fling can be a one-night stand or go on for months, but it is a one-time act of infidelity with no commitment to the new sexual partner. The one-night stand may be perceived as presenting a greater threat to the marriage than it actually does. Although it is painful to discover that a spouse is involved in a fling, you must keep in mind that it is the least serious kind of affair. Ironically, suggests psychiatrist Frank Pittman, it is not because people take infidelity too lightly that a one-night stand may escalate into a more serious matter, but because they take it too seriously.

Consider the following case of Nina and Paul. Our client Nina, a professional woman in her mid-thirties, described such an involvement on a business trip. "I felt so free of responsibility. It was wonderful to just relax on the plane and, finally, stop juggling everything: fixing lunches, cooking, car-pooling, plus my full-time job.

"Paul had agreed to take over for the three days I would be at the convention. We never leave the kids with strangers. I felt a little guilty, but I needed to get away. Whoever said that today's woman would 'have it all' certainly doesn't lead my hectic life. Well, anyway," she continued, "there I was at the conference. It felt wonderful and exciting. I saw this man 'to die for'—broad shouldered and athletic-looking. I couldn't believe it when he came over to me and introduced himself. He said his name was Mark.

"I felt like a schoolgirl. It was thrilling," she said, smiling. "Mark had a good sense of humor and made me laugh in a way that I hadn't done in years. We decided to go down to the cocktail lounge and dance to a live band.

"He was a great dancer, and I hadn't danced in years," Nina continued. "Well, you can guess the rest. He held me close. He listened attentively to any dumb thing I said. Then he kissed me. I knew I should have stopped it, but I couldn't. It was so exciting. I went up to his room," she quietly said.

"We had an exquisitely pleasurable night. Paul and I had been married for twelve years. Nothing like this had ever happened before. I always intended to remain faithful. Paul feels that way too. I was swept away. It felt so good to have a little excitement.

"The next morning when I went back to my room, there was a message from Paul. He had misplaced the address of Kimberley's ballet school, and he wanted me to return his call. That call jolted me back to reality.

"I'm sick over this," Nina cried. "In a flash, I realized how dangerous this could have been. Paul and my daughters mean more to me than any 'exquisitely pleasurable night.'

"I decided not to call or look for Mark. Paul would never forgive me, and I vowed that he would never find out. I am never going to do that again, but I needed to talk to someone about it."

The case of Nina illustrates how a fling can occur when the circumstances are conducive, but it also shows that such an incident can be put into perspective without destroying a marriage.

A fictional illustration of the fling can be found in the film, *Fatal Attraction*, a vivid portrayal that both fascinated and terrified film audiences. In this story, the character played by actor Michael Douglas started what he thought was an innocent flirtation. He soon made the decision to have an affair, intending it to be a fling. He did not take it seriously. In fact, he was happily married to an intelligent and beautiful woman, living well in a posh suburb of New York as a devoted father and respected professional. He had no intention of giving up any of this. He wasn't even looking. His fling, like many others, just happened.

The affair, which had started as an intense flirtation by the woman in question (played by actress Glenn Close) soon became deadly serious because of her frightening behavior. Douglas saw that the fling could not be contained or kept from intruding upon his family or professional life. The marriage went through turmoil from it, and his wife suffered emotionally. However, the marriage did not dissolve. The character played by Michael Douglas was committed to his wife.

President Clinton, in his affair with Monica Lewinsky, came face to face with his own "fatal attraction." The Starr report revealed that Monica Lewinsky was a woman who pursued her man. Lewinsky testified that the affair started as "intense flirting." She said that she had an encounter with him when she wasn't even sure he knew her name. Lewinsky admitted that her attraction to the president later turned to love. Lewinsky testified, "I've always felt that he was sort of my sexual soul mate."

Lewinsky had many bouts of anger when she felt neglected and made demands to see him. Her anger grew, like that of the Glenn Close character in the film, as did her sense of entitlement. In her own words, Ms. Lewinsky said she "went ballistic" when the president had another appointment in the

Oval Office or was playing golf instead of seeing her. She was angry to see news films of the president dancing with the First Lady on a beach vacation. Monica was also enraged at the president's televised "apology" speech following his testimony before the grand jury, because she felt it portrayed her as "providing sexual service" for him.

When she was removed from her job in the White House, she demanded a better job and, as she told the president, "I just wanted it given to me." When this was not immediately forthcoming, she made veiled threats of disclosure, resulting in the president telling her, "It's illegal to threaten the president."

Ms. Lewinsky has been portrayed as a naive young intern, but her testimony showed that she was not so innocent. Ms. Lewinsky testified that at the president's fiftieth birthday party she "playfully touched his crotch" as he passed her while greeting people. Mr. Clinton probably knew he had a "fatal attraction" encounter when, on October 10, 1998, in a telephone conversation, the president told her, "If I had known what kind of person you really were, I wouldn't have gotten involved with you." Unlike the movie character, who was ready to murder, Ms. Lewinsky was protective of the president and testified that she wanted no harm to come to him.

Romantic Love Affairs

We have placed the romantic love affair further along the continuum because it involves a high degree of emotional investment on the part of the lovers. The relationship is very important, and the lovers are concerned about how the affair will be integrated into their lives. What we see most often is that they feel they must either end the affair or divorce and marry the lover. Sometimes a romantic love affair develops from what began as a meaningless fling. The longer the affair continues, the more serious it becomes. Sometimes, when divorce or remarriage is impossible, the romantic love affair can develop into a long-term affair.

Perhaps one of the best-known fictional romantic love affairs is that between Ilsa and Rick in the film *Casablanca*. Rick and Ilsa, lovers before the beginning of World War II, find each other again after the war had separated them. Ilsa is married to Victor Laszlo, a famed resistance hero, when she meets Rick again in Casablanca, and once again they fall in love. But Rick makes the decision that the affair must end and that Ilsa must go off with Victor. The film makes the point that decision-making is an important aspect of such an affair of the heart.

Another affair played out before the ever-watchful eyes of a world audience was that of Prince Charles of England and Camilla Parker Bowles, a married woman. This was a romantic love affair, which Charles gave up when his royal duty called him to marry and produce an heir. Like all romantic love affairs, a decision was made, and Diana became the wife of Prince Charles in 1981. But in 1985, the press began reporting stories about Princess Diana's emotional stress that was seriously affecting her life.

It became apparent that Prince Charles would not honor vows of fidelity to his wife and had resumed his affair with Mrs. Parker Bowles. The troubles of the family were played out in public, and finally Prince Charles divorced Diana. His romantic love affair with Camilla had become a long-term affair. Camilla also obtained a divorce, and she and the Prince admitted they were lovers.

The period preceding and following such a decision is usually difficult and tumultuous. Often the spouse knows of the affair and waits for a decision that affects the very structure of his or her life. To realize that one's spouse loves another is a wrenching experience, whether he leaves or stays. Such heartache was often discussed in our infidelity group.

One of our group members recalled her despair. "I couldn't make sense of it. He tells me, 'I love her. I can't live without her. I am sorry to hurt you, but this is my life. I've got to do it.' What about me?" she asked the group. "Don't I count? *I've* only got one life!"

Another group member replied, "I don't know what's worse. My wife stayed, and I had to watch her grieve for that S.O.B. She cried; she hardly got out of bed. She lost weight. That's not so easy to watch. Maybe it's better they go, and you can start over."

For some, an affair does mean the end of the marriage, but this is not always the case. Marriages can survive to become stronger and monogamous.

Christine, a young aspiring actress, shared the story of her decision to end a love affair. When we first saw her, Christine looked very tired and stressed.

"My husband David has taken a new job in New York with a close friend. I'm supposed to follow him when the summer production I'm acting in is over," she added nervously.

"When rehearsals of the play began, I became attracted to Jeff, a guy in the cast. He's great looking and a talented actor. He's a little younger than I am. It started as a friendship. Now," she sobbed, "I'm having a passionate love affair with him, and I have a husband waiting for me to come to New York. Sex is wonderful with Jeff. The chemistry is there!

"Jeff is so different than my husband David. I met David after a production of *The Crucible*. He's a good looking man, with a beard." She smiled and continued. "He's a little older than me. He had been a professor of English literature at the local Catholic college. He's been a stable influence, but I don't feel the chemical attraction with David. I guess that's the problem. I look up to David and care deeply for him. He's so kind and considerate." She cried when she said this. "What's the matter with me?"

In the weeks that followed her first visit, Christine continued to be very confused. David called her every morning from New York to tell her how much he cared for her. His new job was a little disappointing, but he hoped it would change. He was apartment hunting in preparation for the time she would be joining him.

During this period, Christine agonized over what to do. The summer production was a great success, and secretly Christine hoped that the play would be extended for several more weeks. She didn't want the summer to end. She tried to stall the move by telling David she needed the extra time to pack and take another class.

David became suspicious and asked Christine if she was having an affair. "It was very hard for David to hear it," Christine told us. "I felt like a rat. He was so hurt. He said that he would wait for my decision.

"For a while, I thought of not joining David in New York, but Jeff's a free spirit. He's not ready for a commitment. I know saying good-bye to Jeff would be terribly difficult," Christine concluded. "I can't hurt David. I still care for him. I've decided to end the affair. I'm going to move to New York and work on my marriage. If David loves me and is willing to sacrifice so much for me, he deserves better. I'm going to give him my full commitment."

Long-Term Affairs

At the far end of the continuum is the long-term affair, lasting for years and possibly over the lifetime of the marriage of one of the partners. Like the romantic love affair, the partners feel very emotionally invested. In fact, the long-term affair may have been a romantic love affair in which a decision could not be made. The fact that it lasted so long over the course of the marriage tells us it is formidable. Although you may not have actually agreed to it, if you are married to a spouse so involved, by now you may have accommodated to such a lifestyle. We have seen those involved in a long-term affair feeling more married to the lover than to the marriage partner. A well-known example is that of Katharine Hepburn and Spencer Tracy, who were romantically linked despite the fact that Tracy was married.

As one client told us, "I know, but I look the other way." Others have said, "We discussed it, and I agreed to it." But for most, it is an arrangement by default.

Usually, but not always, a long-term affair is known to families, friends, and, in the case of a celebrity, the public. The longer it goes on, the more likely the spouse is to discover it, or at least to suspect its existence. Some spouses know of the affair but do not care to acknowledge it. This is part of an unspoken contract: "I'll take care of you and be a good spouse, but you must look away so I can have my affair."

In such cases, all three members of the triangle have decided to live with the situation. Some of the reasons include religion, finances, politics, concern for the well-being of the children, and moral objections to divorce.

Religion was an important factor in the case of Keith and Lois. "My husband has been having an affair. It's more than an affair," Lois told us. "I put up with it because of my family and religious values. But I'm miserable. I need help, because I am so depressed." Lois began to cry.

"Keith was the first in his family to go to college," Lois said. "His parents were very proud of him. After graduation, he spent two years as a missionary in a small town in New Zealand. They wouldn't be so proud of him now," Lois said, "but I don't have the heart to tell them. That's part of my problem. I can't tell anyone. Keith has another family.

"Someone wrote me an anonymous letter three years ago," Lois continued, "telling me all about his affair. Keith doesn't deny it. It had been going on for four years before I found out. He tells me Cassie is more fun, and he acts like a father to her kids. It kills me, knowing he buys them Christmas gifts and takes them on vacations. It takes away from our children. He's not going to give her up. He doesn't want a divorce. It's funny. I don't want one either. So we stay together. What we have going now is a sort of package deal. I never thought I'd find myself in a crazy situation like this.

"We make decisions together about the children's education and activities, and I guess I never give up hope that he'll come back to his senses."

Lois became part of a scenario in which her husband had two families because they don't want to be divorced.

Sometimes a spouse may have a long-term affair without the other's knowing anything about it. The truth may not be revealed until after the unfaithful spouse's death. Such a situation came up in our support group when Connie told her story.

Connie explained, "I thought we were happily married for forty years. After Phil died, I was sorting through things to keep or to throw out, and I found papers indicating that he had been having an affair for twelve years.

"There was a checkbook and old statements for an account I didn't know about. Phil made a good income, and it was easy to hide thousands from me. I never was interested in our finances. He evidently paid her rent, gave her a large monthly allowance, and took trips with her."

Connie cried as she continued. "Sometimes I feel shocked all over again. Like hearing it for the first time. A lot of the time I am angry. I feel so torn. He isn't here for me to confront him. I can't ask for explanations. Twelve years is a long time. He must have loved her.

"I don't know why he did it. I feel as though my life with him has been a sham. Everyone thinks he was a saint. And here I am, mixed up because he treated me so well."

Another client, who found records after her husband's death that revealed a long-term affair, was also crushed by the betrayal. However, there was an added twist to her story. She remembered a lifetime of dealing with a chronic shortage of money, and she felt she had sacrificed to make ends meet. But now she discovered that her husband had lavished gifts on his lover and her children, including taking them on expensive vacations. "I was cheated out of my life," she told us.

These cases are not uncommon. Many women find out about their husbands' involvement in long-term affairs after they die. Although frustrated by not being able to confront their spouse, they, too, can come to understand the affair and resolve the crisis.

• • •

Knowing the kind of affair in which your spouse was involved can help you determine its seriousness. Understanding the reasons why it happened provides additional important information to help you make a decision about the future of your marriage.

Chapter 2

Why Affairs Happen

"Is that your wife, or are you on a business trip?"
— Siegfried and Roy, Las Vegas entertainers

"When I first found out that Doug had been cheating on me, I tore myself apart trying to figure out why," Hildy told the group. "I was furious at him," she continued, "but then I came down hard on myself. I know the woman Doug was involved with. I was surprised she wasn't this siren type or femme fatale. I couldn't understand it, but I tried hard to improve myself. I got a perm, I had manicures, I exercised, I tried to read more, to cook gourmet meals, to be more charming, to be sexy—everything I could think of to be better. What's wrong with me?"

"Nothing is wrong with you," was the response of her group.

"Then why?" Hildy asked.

People experiencing the kind of pain that Hildy feels usually search for understanding. They often think, "Something's wrong with me," or "The sex is better with her." Because infidelity involves sex, many mistakenly assume that better sex is the motivation for the affair. Sometimes this is true, but most of the time it isn't. Another assumption people make is that something is wrong with the marriage. Again, this is often the case, but we have also seen infidelity in good marriages. As one woman in a recent group said of a betrayed spouse, "Evidently she wasn't meeting his needs." In some cases, those needs may be completely at odds with the marriage. This is the case when there is a need to maintain distance from a spouse and avoid intimacy.

One couple came to us for counseling because they had difficulty communicating and making decisions. But the relationship failed to improve after they learned better skills. She felt something was wrong but couldn't put her finger on it. "It feels like there is a barrier between us," she told us.

In an individual session with the husband, he admitted having a private life of seeing prostitutes, but he claimed that he did not have sex with them but only fondled and played. However, he repeatedly sought prostitutes or picked up women at bars, even though he claimed he loved his wife, and they both agreed they had a great sex life together.

People are likely to cheat for many reasons. Some reasons are individual and have nothing to do with their marriage, although a spouse may have looked to their marriage with the expectation that it would solve those problems.

When coauthor Rona Subotnik was a guest on the *Leeza* television talk show, one of the guests told the audience that he didn't know it was damaging to his marriage to have an affair because everyone in his family had them. The audience "booed" him when he made this statement. They then cheered the author when she told him he would have to take responsibility for his behavior.

Behavior can be repeated throughout generations in a family. That is why, for example, mental health professionals feel that a history of suicide in a family is a "risk factor" when assessing a person for suicide.

Applying this generational view to families, we need only look at the many affairs in the Kennedy family. The message for this family has been that having extramarital affairs is acceptable behavior for the male. The females, however, are expected to tolerate it, and they have. Rose Kennedy did just this during the long relationship her husband had with Gloria Swanson and his many other affairs. Her daughters-in-law responded to their husbands' affairs in the same way, just as Rose Kennedy's mother did, when her father, John Fitzgerald, had an affair with "Toodles" Ryan.

When we hear of the close relationship between N.C. Wyeth and his daughter-in-law, Caroline, as reported in David Michaelis' book, *N.C. Wyeth, A Biography*, we can't help but think of N.C. Wyeth's son, Andrew, and his "involvement with model Helga Testorf." Andrew Wyeth kept this secret from his wife, Betsy, for fifteen years, during which time the famous "Helga" paintings were created.

Perhaps the most dramatic generational display of such a family pattern was the affair of Mrs. Alice Keppel with King Edward VII of England. This same pattern was repeated many years later when Camilla Parker Bowles, Keppel's great-granddaughter, had an affair with Edward's great-grandson, Prince Charles.

A family history of extramarital affairs is not a cause of infidelity. We believe the reason for infidelity lies with the personal problems of one or both individuals, or problems within the marriage. Working with families, we have seen that family stresses, critical life changes, unresolved personal problems, and losses can reverberate throughout the family with many possible responses. If affairs have occurred in the family before, it is quite possible under these conditions that this behavior could be repeated. Individuals who come from a family with a history of infidelity may try to resolve their problems by having affairs because that becomes a familiar option. The individual may not even be aware of this influence. As one woman told us, "The whole damned family screwed around, but I thought Pierre was different. And he was, until we filed for bankruptcy. Then he became just like his father and brothers."

Transitional Anxiety

It is our belief that most extramarital involvement occurs from anxiety arising from individual or family transitions. Like individuals, families go through developmental stages. The anxiety that occurs in making the transition from one life stage to the next, whether it is an individual or a family one, is one reason people choose to be unfaithful.

Psychologist Nancy Schlossberg tells us that a transition is "an event or non-event resulting in a change of assumptions about oneself and the world." Although we think of transitions as something new that happens, a transition can actually be something that doesn't happen, such as the child that cannot be conceived, the professional aspirations that will not be realized, or the status that cannot be reached. All of these can generate transition anxiety. From this expanded view of a transition we are able to recognize that stress can occur even when there is no apparent external event.

Transitional life events include both losses, like death, separation, and divorce, and positive occurrences, like marriage, the birth of a baby, and job promotion. With every transition there is a loss. We lose a role or a view of ourselves, and with it the comfort of understanding what was formerly expected of us. Change brings not just a new role but the anxieties that come with new expectations and responsibilities.

It is during such transitions that infidelity is most apt to occur. The prospective bride or bridegroom, although not yet married, may have an affair—often looked at in the conventional wisdom as a "last fling." More likely, it is caused by anxiety over the approaching marriage.

It is also not unusual for therapists to see cases of fathers having affairs at the time a child is born. This is hard for many people to understand. The birth of a child is a positive event, one that people believe should bring happiness, and so they are surprised to find it precipitates an estrangement. In reality, the unfaithful spouse is acting on the anxiety that comes with new expectations and responsibilities. This is a stressful time, with many things happening. To begin with, new mothers are very focused on the almost constant demands of the baby, and they are usually very tired with little time or energy left for the husband.

Mothers of newborns may also be going through emotional "ups and downs" as a result of hormonal changes, a normal but often stressful biological phenomenon. A first-time father may be quite stunned by these changes, and he may think that his importance is reduced. He may even feel rejected by his wife's lack of attention. A veteran dad may be prepared for these occurrences but still feel resentful.

For some new fathers a newborn means adult responsibility for the first time. They are required to grow up. This can be very frightening to someone who feels he is not up to the challenge. For some fathers the anxiety is so acute that they cope by having sex with someone else. Interestingly, no case of infidelity receives as much scorn as that of the father of a newborn, except perhaps the spouse who cheats on a dying mate.

Judging from the number of cases seen in our office, the midlife crisis is one of the major developmental stages during which infidelity occurs. Midlife is a pivotal time for both men and women. It is a time when individuals feel the ticking of the clock, a time of evaluation of a life half over.

Midlife evaluation is not easy. Psychologist Daniel Levinson, who studied the effect of midlife evaluations in men, reported that it was a time of major turmoil in a man's life. Our experience has shown that it is a very anxious time for women as well.

Although this process of introspection is uncomfortable, it is also a productive way to set priorities and goals. Such evaluations are done in all areas of life: marriage, career, lifestyle, friendships, and interests. On the other hand, the pain of "looking inward" creates anxiety, and many people attempt to deal with their midlife crisis by having an affair. Usually this affair is merely a diversion or distraction from taking stock, the main event.

Far from providing a true solution to the individual's problems, the affair solves nothing. And it is an unfortunate choice because of the pain it causes others. Moreover, it postpones or prevents the real work of making plans for the second half of life, which is what a midlife crisis is really all about. Many people leave a marriage at this stage of life, marry the new person, and later discover that they are no happier since the real solution lies elsewhere.

Other major family lifecycle events that cause stress occur in raising teenagers, coping with aging parents, and launching children in

independent living. Take the first, raising adolescents. This has histori-
cally been a trying task. Most families who seek family therapy do so
when their children are adolescents. Some spouses, overwhelmed by the
stress in the family and tired of seeking solutions to problems, seek
escape in an affair.

When the children are teenagers, parents are usually in their own
midlife years. Thus, the restlessness of the midlife crisis often coincides
with the strife of the teenage years. Since the advances of medical science
have lengthened the life span, parents may at the same time be dealing with
their own aging parents and the problems that their parents' infirmities
bring. Such situations have become so commonplace that the term "the
sandwich generation" has been coined to describe the conflict. When
everything in life seems to be going wrong, an affair may appear to offer an
escape, a break from the problems, and comfort. It is a false solution.

A death in the family is another life event that often strains a relationship and makes it vulnerable to infidelity. In our practices, we have seen
that marriages have difficulty accommodating the loss of a child. We
remember one case in which the father became involved after the death of
his daughter with a single woman who had a child.

The aging process, another life transition, can cause stress as one sees
the years dwindling and sadly notices undesired changes in the body. Some
people have plastic surgery, some become "exercise freaks," and others
have affairs. Many extramarital involvements are entered into as a reassur-
ance against the aging process. Indeed, as the population at large gets older,
we become more aware that the elderly also have affairs, though for many
it is a shock to see a senior "stepping out." We know from listening to their
stories that an older person's unfaithfulness may be an attempt to ward off
feelings of depression from growing older. Unfortunately, such a solution
is an emotional "whistling in the dark."

The world of the impotent male, most of whom are in the older age
category, was rocked in March of 1998 when the anti-impotence pill,
Viagra, was authorized for sale in the United States. In the period from
March through the middle of September of that year, the manufacturer of
the pill reported that Viagra had been prescribed to more than 4 million
American men.

Obviously, the alchemists of the Middle Ages were on the wrong trail
to finding gold. Immediately, there were reports that men in European
nations began clamoring for the drug, and Japanese businessmen began fly-
ing to the States to buy and sell one of the most sought-after drugs ever to
be marketed.

The use of Viagra affects married couples in profound ways. Although many devoted couples who had adjusted to the lack of sex in their lives were thrilled at its return, some of the early reports were not as rosy. Some couples separated, and some men started having affairs after they began to use the pill.

It is quite common in our society for an aging male to cope with his fears by finding a younger woman. The excitement of an affair may make him feel younger and less anxious. We do not see older women having affairs with the same frequency as men. It is not that the aging woman is free of this anxiety, quite the contrary. However, in our society, the option to seek a younger lover is less available to aging women because of a pervasive gender bias in our culture and because of negative stereotyping of the older woman. These factors not only make her less sought-after as a sexual partner but also significantly lower her self-esteem. In addition, there are fewer males than females in this age group, and the males are generally looking for younger women. We have heard women talk about aging as something shameful.

Consider the case of Sharon, who came for counseling because of the stress she was feeling from what she termed her "home situation."

"Ten months ago," she began, "I discovered I had genital warts, and had to get painful medical treatments. I found out that my husband, Felix, was having an affair. He told me he was having an affair with a young woman named Trisha, a graduate student at the university where he works.

"I've really been a fool," she cried. "He told me he needed 'space' for a while. I can't believe I bought that, but I did. He said he would leave if he didn't get his 'space.'

"I agreed, but I couldn't eat, sleep, or concentrate. I asked him to go with me for therapy, but he refused. He said it was my problem. So we are separating while he dates Trisha.

"You know, this probably sounds stupid to you, but Felix has never had an affair before. He's been a devoted family man and a well-respected faculty member of the university. This is not in keeping with his personality. We have a lot going for us—five terrific kids, money, a home, and lots of friends.

"Felix is sixty, and he is going to retire soon. I thought he was depressed. He always wanted to write a book. He talked of missed opportunities and disappointments. I thought there was still time for him to write the book. We had planned retirement together.

"Now I'm a fifty-five-year-old woman looking for work. They're calling me a 'displaced homemaker.' Do you know how horrible that sounds to me? But I *am* displaced. At fifty-five I have to find a new life, and I have a disease to deal with."

Sharon's husband was having an affair at a critical time in his life, as he was facing retirement. He probably began this affair as a way for him to fight off the demons he saw in aging. His wife was a reminder of his aging, and he labeled her "old and fat." The problems were not in their marriage but in his own personal concerns.

Transitions are anxious times for all of us. Successful transitions depend on our strengths, supports, and resources. It's a time of vulnerability when infidelity can become a way, albeit an ineffective one, of dealing with the anxiety.

Unfulfilled Expectations

When people marry, they do so with the expectation that they will be happy and have a satisfying emotional and sexual life, with many of their needs met by their partner.

Many of these expectations are part of a contract couples enter into. In his description of the marriage contract, psychiatrist Clifford Sager writes that couples make a contract on three levels of awareness. The first level is the verbalized, in which they speak their agreement to each other. The vows spoken at the wedding ceremony are an example of an agreement at this level.

The second level of contract is not verbalized. For example, the husband expects that his wife will not criticize him in public, although he has not said this to her. The third level of the marriage contract is beyond awareness, and so it is harder for either of them to know.

These agreements are very significant because they are dictated by our emotional needs; thus, our feeling of well-being is based on them. Expectations may be unrealistic or altered by time and personal growth, leading to a change in the agreement. As with any contract, it is essential that both parties be willing to change and to renegotiate. If both parties are not in agreement, the contract is broken. One or the other may behave in certain ways, such as arguing, withdrawing, becoming anxious or depressed, or drawing others into the picture. Infidelity is one way of drawing another into the situation.

An example of such an arrangement is the contract, which may occur on any one of the three levels, that says, "Take care of me in this complex and bewildering world, and in return you can make the decisions." The payoff for the dependent spouse is security; for the other, increased self-esteem. As usual in this kind of contract, a shift somewhere can make a delicately balanced agreement collapse. The wife may become more assertive and want more independence, upsetting the balance. This frequently happens at midlife. She may decide to start a business or go to school. If this doesn't fit in with his view of the contract, then their agreement is breached. Her husband may become anxious as he sees her excel at business, feeling his expertise is needed less and less.

We have seen broken contracts when one spouse becomes more well-known or makes more money than the other in a common field of work. If this upsets the equilibrium of their contract, then the resulting tension could lead to an affair by one or the other.

Sometimes a dependent spouse becomes dissatisfied with the power she had originally given over to her husband, especially if he has become excessively controlling. When the wife rebels, the husband's expectations are not fulfilled, and as far as he is concerned the original contract is broken. If the rebellion cannot be easily tolerated by the controlling partner, the husband may act out his resentment in the form of an affair, or the wife may look elsewhere for sympathy and understanding.

In a case where the contract requires one spouse to be responsible for the happiness and well-being of the other, the deal may be too difficult to uphold. Some contracts are broken when one spouse violates the agreement, which may or may not be verbalized, regarding emotional distance between the partners. For example, when one spouse demands more closeness, the partner who needs "space" may become anxious and distant. The distancing could take the form of an affair. It is impossible to have emotional closeness or intimacy with a spouse and have an affair at the same time.

Sarah and Henry were such a couple. They came to therapy because Sarah had had an affair, and he was furious. Their arguments brought them into therapy.

"I changed her world," Henry told us with great feeling. "I gave her stability after her divorce from her first husband. He was a jerk. They were both too immature for marriage."

"It's true," Sarah took up the story. "When I met Henry, I was going to college at night and working during the day. I was going to be the first college graduate in my family. My family didn't understand or support me in this.

"I was attracted to Henry by his good looks," she continued. "He was getting his MBA, and his future looked bright. He liked my lively nature, and he was flattered by my interest in him. We got married, and I supported both of us while Henry got his degree."

Sarah told us, "I was a damn good mother. I went to PTA meetings. I was a Cub Scout mom. I drove car pools. Everybody thought I had a perfect life."

"But things were not good," Henry said. "We argued. I couldn't please her. She called me a 'wimp.' I was too quiet. Even with my MBA, I couldn't make enough money for the things she wanted."

As they told us more, we could feel Henry's helplessness and Sarah's anger. For him, Sarah's liveliness had turned to "bitchiness." He could never measure up to her expectations. Sarah was disappointed that he never took the initiative. He didn't make dinner plans or buy her surprise gifts. Henry was aware that he fell short of her expectations of him.

Sarah started working. Even though her salary allowed them to have a better home, new furniture, a new car, designer clothes, travel, and more entertainment, the anger she felt toward Henry for not keeping his part of the unspoken contract was not abated.

It was at this point in their marriage that Sarah became involved with another man at work. She told us, "I didn't know what I wanted."

Henry and Sarah continued to work together on their marriage. Sarah had some individual work to do in order to understand why she placed these unrealistic expectations on Henry. Sarah had brought her own self-esteem issues into the marriage; she was trying to find self-esteem through someone else. In her contract, she wanted status and a take-charge man, and Henry could never earn enough or be bold enough for her. In fact, she did view him as a "wimp" instead of appreciating his predictability and stability. Sarah had lived up to Henry's expectations of her to be a devoted mother. However, she had broken the unspoken contract between them in regard to the issue of respect by treating him poorly. She was to be the lively dynamo of the family, but her liveliness took an unpleasant turn when she became disappointed in Henry.

Individual expectations can change in the course of a marriage, as people develop new interests and learn more about themselves. Generally, they can become incorporated into a marriage without any repercussions. When, however, the change is dramatically different from the way the couple has been conducting their lives all along, the equilibrium of the marriage can be greatly disturbed.

An example of such a case was Jacob and Rose, who came in for counseling about Jacob's flirtation and intense friendship with their neighbor,

Lila. Although Jacob never had sex with Lila, he admitted that he desired her, and he knew this obsession with her threatened his marriage.

Jacob had developed a strong interest in becoming more Orthodox in his practice of Judaism. This is not an interest that one member could participate in alone because it is a way of life with strict religious practices and standards. It requires the work, support, and involvement of the wife. Rose would be obligated to keep a kosher home and carefully observe the rules of Sabbath. There would be a prohibition against previous activities, such as men and women dancing together. As a busy lawyer, Rose found it hard to accept, and there were many arguments about her "level of commitment and sabotaging" his needs. Jacob said that his religious scruples kept him from having sexual relations with Lila, but this attitude meant little to Rose. She viewed his relationship with Lila to be "an affair."

Jacob found he was getting more understanding from Lila than from Rose. However, in their counseling sessions, each of them learned to listen to the other's needs and problems. Eventually, they became more understanding and supportive of each other.

Need for Attention

Although it may strike readers as dramatic or extreme, one partner in the relationship may sometimes become unfaithful as a way of getting the attention of the other. In these affairs the unfaithful spouse wants to change some unbearable aspect of the relationship rather than end the marriage. The purpose of the affair is to bring attention to the situation when previous attempts have failed.

The "need for attention" results from poor communication. Partners are not able to tell each other what they want or pay attention to the expressed desires of the other. This affair occurs out of frustration. It is a way of saying, "I can't communicate with you in any other way."

Such was the case of Claudette and Ralph, who have been married for fifteen years and have a thirteen-year-old son, Joshua. Joshua is developmentally disabled. They came for marriage therapy after Ralph realized that Claudette had been unfaithful.

Claudette began by discussing her son. "Joshua is a very lovable little boy. We are very close." Ralph quickly interrupted. "I think that's part of the problem. She's overly involved. They're too close. That's how her damn affair started with that guy from the association, and she's always working on something with those people."

Claudette explained, "Ralph is talking about Harry, the ex-director of the state program. I've worked with him on many committees. He understands what I am going through."

"And I don't?" Ralph shouted. "I am the boy's father, for God's sake!"

Claudette and Ralph began to argue. She accused Ralph of being cold, remote, and unsympathetic to Joshua's problems. Because of her involvement with Joshua, Claudette has been unable to maintain friends or other interests. In fact, without the community of those involved with developmental disabilities, she feels she would have no friends, no one who understands her.

In their counseling sessions, Claudette and Ralph began to talk honestly with each other. We then began to understand the dynamics of this triangle. When Joshua's diagnosis was made, shortly after his birth, Ralph was stoic in his acceptance. In fact, he did not allow himself to grieve for the hopes and dreams that he had secretly held for his newborn son. Although his heart was broken, just as Claudette's was, he threw himself into his work. Claudette felt this as distancing and rejecting. She became depressed and dealt with her depression by involving herself completely with her son and his world.

Now Claudette and Ralph were given the opportunity to cry together and comfort each other and also to release their anger. With this work accomplished, they were both free to love Joshua and to be sharing parents in his life. Ralph could resume his role of parent and free Claudette from assuming the whole burden. With Ralph's support, Claudette could develop herself and her other interests and still be the parent she wants to be to Joshua.

Although the problems she faced were quite serious, changes are possible. You can see from this case how an affair can develop in a marriage where two people care about each other but are unable to communicate their problems. The affair serves as a very dramatic way to get attention, to solve the problem, and to continue with their relationship.

Boredom

Affairs may also occur when partners become bored with each other. We often hear the phrase from our clients, "I've outgrown her." We know that adults continue to grow and develop throughout the life span. Our longer life span now insures that couples will spend more years together than ever before.

Opportunities in education, travel, recreation, and entertainment are more available to this generation than to those in the past. The opportunity to grow can create boredom and stress in a relationship if one partner seizes these opportunities and the other does not. The results can be boredom in the marriage and anger at the partner for not keeping up. When such dissatisfaction exists, it leaves a marriage vulnerable to infidelity.

Jack and Mary, a couple who came for counseling, were good examples of this kind of marriage. They said that they had been having marital problems for years. They had separated three times and were on the verge of another separation when they came for marriage counseling.

Mary was very attractive and animated. Jack was handsome, quiet, and polite. Mary began. "We were high school sweethearts. We lived on the same block in a small town in Oklahoma. We started dating when we were fourteen years old and got married after high school. Jack joined the Army, and we both left home for the first time. Army life was great. I worked in a department store. The Army sent Jack to college to study engineering. Our families were very proud of us. They thought we had everything—Jack's college education, a family, a home—and when Jack left the Army he got a good job as an engineer in Baltimore.

"Actually, things were terrible. Jack picked on me all the time. He criticized and found fault with everything, from the food I served to the color I painted the kitchen. Almost every family outing ended in a fight."

Mary cried as she continued. "We began our separations about the time that our youngest child, Carole, started school. But Jack kept coming back. He said he missed the family."

Jack told us that college had opened up worlds he had not seen while growing up. He found courses in art, theater, and music to be very exciting, and he wanted Mary to learn more about them. Mary was not interested in attending concerts and ballets or in going to art exhibits and plays. Jack wouldn't attend without her.

"I grew bored," he revealed. "We had grown apart. About the only thing we talked about were the children and the routine business of running the house. I felt I no longer wanted to be married to her. If it weren't for the kids, I would have left."

It seemed to us that the distance between them had grown each year. Jack's anger at Mary for not joining him in his interests became displaced, and it was inappropriately expressed as criticism of her methods of child rearing and housekeeping. Jack felt that they had nothing in common, only the children to keep them together.

Mary did not know, however, that Jack was having an affair. On a business trip to New York, where Jack was assigned to an engineering project, he began to have an affair with a woman he met at a bar. Even though Jack saw her every time he went to New York, he wanted his marriage to work. He didn't want to be a weekend father, so he asked Mary to see a marriage counselor with him. She readily agreed because she was so unhappy. In their counseling session, Jack revealed his affair to Mary. Mary was not surprised, but she was angry nevertheless.

Clearly, this was a marriage characterized by boredom. Couples can grow apart as one of the pair expands his or her world and the other stands still. Jack and Mary continued to work out their feelings about the affair and then to understand what had happened to them over the years. Mary really wanted to join Jack in his world, but her low self-esteem immobilized her. We worked on strategies to change her attitudes and to build her confidence. Jack became aware of why he criticized her and how this reinforced her poor self-image. Jack and Mary were able to work this out together and remain married.

The Unavailable Spouse

Sometimes a spouse is emotionally and sexually unavailable to the partner, usually because of physical or mental illness, geographical distance, or military service. For some people these are not justifications to break a "till death do us part" commitment, but infidelity does occur under such circumstances.

Military service often separates couples, sometimes for long periods. Many a G.I. who received a "Dear John" letter can attest to the strain that physical separation placed on a relationship.

Until recently, we have come to expect that the affair occurs with the spouse who remains at home, but military service is changing dramatically. Women are playing different roles in the services today. For example, during the Gulf War, in many cases women fought beside men. Women are involved all the way up the ranks, often in leadership positions. They are blazing new trails as fighter pilots and ship captains. When men and women are working side by side, sharing a stressful and dangerous experience in often depressing environments and away from their usual support, the conditions exist for them to turn to one another for comfort and for sex.

The spouse who is not able to have sex because of physical or mental illness also deprives the other of marital companionship and support.

Consider the story of Benjamin and Janice, who started their marriage with a firm belief in the sanctity of their wedding vows. Neither believed that the other would, or could, be unfaithful, so deep was their trust for one another. Despite this beginning, their lives took a completely unexpected course. It was Ellen, the other woman, who told us the story.

"Janice and Ben were married," she began, "after Ben graduated from college. Janice supported them while Ben got his Ph.D. in psychology. He told me things were going well in the early years. He had a private practice, and Janice went back to school to become a teacher. They had three healthy children.

"He said he felt so lucky," she continued. "But just after their tenth anniversary, Janice's problems began. First she started to have small automobile accidents. Then she began to limp and to drop things. They went to one doctor after another and had lots of tests. Some were painful. Then they found out that Janice had multiple sclerosis.

"She's been in a wheelchair for five years now. If you have to have something as awful as MS, you should have a husband like Ben. He's a saint. He takes her shopping and to the theater. Although it was difficult for them both, they've even gone to Europe, Hawaii, and cruised the Caribbean.

"I met Ben in a stress management support group," Ellen went on. "I had really been stressed out from my divorce, and my life with that crumb of a husband. I mean my ex, I should say. Well, anyhow, the leader talked about how helpful hobbies are for stress. So three of us from the group took a photography class. Ben was part of the group. We started going for coffee after class.

"Ben is so sweet," she told us. "It was wonderful to be with him—so different than my ex. So we began an affair. It's been going on for a year. I love Ben. He's a wonderful man. But he can't sort out his feelings. He's happy with me and delighted to be having a sex life, but he feels a competing duty to Janice. In a way, I can understand it," she said sadly.

We could understand it also. Ben still cared for his wife and cherished the investment that they had made in each other. Ben and Ellen could not go on like this. They were coming to a decision as many couples do in a romantic love affair. They were ending their affair.

Lack of Sexual Desire

When one or both partners experience a lack of sexual desire, the relationship may be vulnerable to the temptations of sex with someone else. There are many reasons for a lack of sexual desire, including sexual dysfunction. Sex therapy has been very successful in treating these conditions. Sometimes reduced sexual interest develops from attitudes that couples have developed throughout their years of marriage, as well as carryovers from childhood. When sex becomes a duty, it ceases to be fun or erotic, and some react by avoiding it.

One common complaint that we hear from women is that they want their spouses to show more affection. There are often significant differences between women and men in this regard. Women want tenderness, hugs, and cuddling at times other than when they are in bed. They want to feel that they are valued by their husbands at all times, not just when it is time for sex.

As one client told us, "Some sign of tenderness—a touch, a kiss, a hand on my waist earlier in the day—is all I ask. Men don't understand that's part of foreplay. It's like that song, 'Give me a kiss to build a dream on.'"

This expectation on the part of the woman may become a problem for the man. We remember our client, Leon, who said, "I feel awkward after she tells me to touch her. It feels phony. She ought to know I love her. I'm there, aren't I?" In his view that was sufficient evidence of his feeling for his wife.

On the other hand, men often feel that they are not heard by their wives when they request more sensuality. They may desire more passion and eroticism in their lovemaking. They complain that their wives feel uncomfortable experimenting with anything out of the ordinary, and the ordinary has become routine. When these stalemates arise, they begin to avoid sex with each other.

This was the case with Sally, who came to our office in tears. Four months earlier Sally had discovered that Herb was having an affair. It had not been going on very long before she suspected and confronted him.

"He cried," Sally told us. "I was really surprised," she continued. "He cried a lot. He said he didn't know why it happened. He told me over and over again that he loved me."

Tensions were high between Sally and Herb, however, even after the fling ended. Sally came alone for therapy. The therapist asked Herb to join Sally so that they could work on their problems together. First they had to deal with Sally's emotions of rage and disappointment, feelings of betrayal, and lack of trust before understanding why the infidelity had occurred.

A story began to unravel of a very responsible and overworked wife and mother of three children. She saw her husband's desire for more fun in bed as another responsibility. She was not enjoying it and began making excuses to avoid it. Sex did not seem to fit in with her view of herself as a serious, dependable mother and wife.

It seemed that Sally was responsible for the family's financial affairs. In fact, she suspected the affair from paying the bills. She had noticed some gift charges, phone calls to another zone, and an unexplained increase in gasoline charges, and she decided "something was fishy."

Herb's fling was meaningless in the sense that he had no emotional investment in the other woman. So the couple began to work toward a solution by dividing the household chores more evenly and by adjusting Sally's schedule to allow for more free time. Sally needed permission to lighten up and have some fun. They also started working on experiencing sexual pleasure in each other through pleasuring exercises. In time, Sally told us with a smile, "This is more fun than I thought it would be, too."

Poor-Risk Partners

Another reason for infidelity is that one spouse is a poor-risk partner. The poor-risk partner is most likely to have serial affairs or one-night stands. Many such partners have serious personality problems, often with a long history of poor interpersonal relationships starting in childhood. In fact, his history may be one of having erratic and stormy relationships with family members, bosses, friends, and members of the opposite sex.

Some poor-risk partners are very self-absorbed; they have a constant need for admiration. They view all events narcissistically in terms of the events impact on them. Their behavior is often impulsive. These individuals may be completely lacking in empathy, unable to see anything from another person's viewpoint. They cannot accept criticism, and often their egos require constant bolstering. This behavior is more than a lack of self-esteem. It goes to the very core of the individual's personality and is a pervasive aspect of his lifestyle. This personality flaw prevents them from keeping marriage vows.

A narcissistic person cannot put himself in the place of another and understand the other person's feelings. So the depths of despair of the betrayed spouse means nothing to the infidel. Empathy is essential to resolving issues of infidelity.

One woman who came for therapy with her husband, because of his affair, told of how he went to a business meeting rather than accompany her to her father's funeral. He did the same thing when his daughter threatened suicide. The needs of his family and the suffering of his wife made little difference to him. He left his wife—typical of him—at New Year's Eve.

Other poor-risk partners are those who are addicted to sex and seem unable to control their need to have excitement and new partners in their lives. They go from lover to lover, unable to achieve intimacy, and are incapable of commitment. Poor-risk partners are usually unable to make an emotional commitment, and it is useless to expect it from them.

Patrick Carnes, an authority on sexual addiction, defines it as "a pathological relationship, in which sexual obsession replaces people. . . . The core belief is that sex is the most important need." Carnes says that the addict is sustained by excitement and becomes, like the alcoholic, completely absorbed with his addiction. Carnes recognizes three levels of addiction. The first includes commonly accepted behaviors, only they are done compulsively. The second level involves illegal behaviors, and the third level, behaviors that victimize, such as rape.

Although most addicts do not recognize it, according to Carnes, their addiction is rooted in anger. The excitement and the trance-like feeling present during the sexual behavior blocks the anger and, thus, their psychic pain.

Sexual addiction interferes with work, family, and enjoyment of life. Psychologist Dr. Don-David Lusterman says it is "high-risk behavior, and the risk-taking is part of the addictive high. . . . The addict is ashamed of his or her behavior, and therefore becomes a skilled liar."

Many of the issues associated with sexual addiction are similar to those of other addictions, such as alcoholism. The family members become enmeshed in the addict's behavior. Some therapists believe the wife is codependent, that is, adopting behavior that protects him, and thus plays a part in allowing his addiction to continue. This, we believe, is often an unfair assessment of the situation. In reality, it is not so black and white an issue for many families, as the label of codependent portrays. As in other addictions, the person with the problem is responsible for his behavior. No one else is. Sexual addicts need treatment, as does the family, because behavior of one family member affects that of the other members. Additionally, sexual addicts usually have more than one addiction.

How can we tell whether serial lovers are sex addicts or philanderers? According to psychologist Shirley Glass, sexual addicts are driven by a compulsion to relieve their tension and anxiety by their extramarital sexual behavior. By contrast, a philanderer takes sex when it is available.

President Clinton's sexual encounters with Monica Lewinsky were extremely reckless behavior, since they occurred in a busy office environment, often with the door partly opened. The chance of being detected was great. Even harder for many people to comprehend was the risk to his presidency. The president said that he was sorry for this involvement and even stopped it for many months, but eventually allowed the affair to continue. According to Monica Lewinsky, "he (the president) didn't want to get addicted to me, and he didn't want me to get addicted to him."

Dick Morris, former presidential adviser, testified before the grand jury that he called the president after reading accounts of the Lewinsky matter. Mr. Clinton confided to Morris, "You know, ever since the election, I've tried to shut myself down. I tried to shut my body down sexually, I mean. . . . But sometimes, I slipped up with this girl. I just slipped up."

This is not the first time that the American public learned of presidential infidelity. In 1998, many public television stations aired "The President's Collection." The special program on the Kennedys explored the sexual appetites of President John F. Kennedy. Priscilla McMillan, a staff member for Kennedy when he was a senator, reported her conversation with him as follows: "Jack, when you are straining every gasket to be elected president, why do you endanger it by going out with women? He thought about it and replied, 'Because I just can't help it.'"

Dick Morris also indulged in high-risk behavior by having a long-term affair with a prostitute and allowing her to listen to his confidential phone conversations with President Clinton. When this became known, Morris resigned his position. The public also soon learned that he had fathered a child as a result of another affair.

Are famous or powerful men more prone to having affairs? From our observation, it appears that the answer is yes. Women are attracted to successful men, such as entertainers, athletes, politicians, and presidents. As one well-known athlete told us, "It's thrown at me. I walk into a hotel lobby and they come over and flirt with me." It doesn't mean that every woman who is in contact with such a man will have an affair, nor will every successful man. But enough do to make us take notice.

Does success make a man a high-risk partner? Opportunity may knock more often for him, but he doesn't necessarily answer.

Not all poor-risk partners are famous people. An example of this kind of partner is Greg, the husband of our client, Candy. Candy is now raising their child alone as a single parent. She grew up as an only child in a middle-class family. "I think my troubles started in junior high school," Candy told us. "My parents were very strict. I started to hang around with the 'wrong' crowd at school. I wore too much makeup, cut class a lot. I know I was smart, but I didn't apply myself," she admitted.

"I met Greg in my freshman year at State," she told us. "He lived off campus in a trailer. He was different from anyone I had ever met.

"I spent a lot of time in his trailer. Greg worked part-time at a gas station. We became lovers. My grades fell, and at the end of my second semester I found out I was pregnant. Greg was furious. He wanted me to have an abortion, but I refused. When I was five months pregnant, Greg agreed to marry me.

"I was delighted," she told us. "I even thought it might work. I dropped out of school. After the baby was born, Greg became even more irresponsible, drinking and doing drugs. All the work and troubles fell on my shoulders.

"When somebody called and told me he was 'messing around' with a woman at a bar, I really started to evaluate my life. I've been screwing up, and I decided to stop. I wanted to get my life together. I asked Greg to leave. I knew that being a single parent would be difficult, but I want to have a better life for me and my daughter. I came here to try to understand how I got myself into this mess and ended up with Greg."

Many women, like Candy, have decided to stop blaming themselves and invest their energies in understanding why they married a poor-risk partner.

An Affair with a Purpose

Occasionally an affair happens when a personal goal is desired. Many of these affairs are for professional or social advancement. As our client Regina, a junior accountant, explained to us, "I guess I was sleeping my way to the top. I knew it was wrong, but at the same time I felt I would never get my career going if I didn't. It's a hard field, especially for women, to get into. What I didn't expect was the effect it had on other parts of my life. I thought I could handle it. I thought my husband would never suspect. Unfortunately, he did, and he was so angry he filed for divorce. I've paid a high price. In my book, no job is worth it."

There are times that the purpose of an affair is to seek revenge or to retaliate when a spouse has had an affair or a series of them. Marla told the group that she later realized this was her motive. "I'll show him," she thought. "I'll let him know how it feels to think about your partner kissing and making love to another. Let him sit up all night imagining the love scenes, like I have done.

"However, I am sorry now," she continued. "I realized I acted out of anger and a wish to see him hurt. My desire for revenge was so great that I couldn't think of the consequences of my actions or another way to stop his affairs. It really isn't the way to solve such problems. I felt bad about myself, like what I did was come down to his level."

The Family Affair

The family affair deserves special attention because it involves a betrayal that cuts to the core of special relationships. In this case the spouse becomes sexually involved with a family member who is a relative by marriage. It is not incest because the extramarital involvement is not with a blood relation. Although this is not a common kind of affair, we have seen it in marriages of both long and short duration and believe it to be the most lethal of all affairs. It has a ripple effect that reaches out and creates pain to many members of the family.

Basic family therapy teaches us that the family system acts as a unit, and when one member defects and takes sides with an outsider, it amounts to family treason. In the case of infidelity, it is extremely painful to see solemn vows taken with one family member broken in order to have sex with another. The chasm within the family becomes deep and often impossible to heal. It places family members in positions they find impossible, making issues of loyalty and betrayal intensely felt.

One case of a family affair came to our attention when Nola came for therapy with her parents. All three were distraught over the situation they found themselves in. Nola began by saying, "I feel as though I am living in a soap opera.

"Chris and I began to have problems after a few years of marriage. Chris was cool, and even rude, to me. Our sex life was zilch. I told my sister, Mary, that Chris might be having an affair. That turned out to be pretty stupid." Nola's mother reached out to touch her hand as she continued to dab her tearful eyes. "One evening, in a talk I had with Chris, he repeated almost verbatim something I had told Mary. I was stunned. I realized that Chris was having an affair with my own sister! He admitted it, too. They wanted to get married. Can you believe it?"

"I could kill him," Nola's father said. "He's ruined everyone's life. My wife and me. Nola. The kids. His parents. He betrayed us all.

"How can we ever accept that bastard as our son-in-law with our second daughter? How can we ever celebrate Christmas and Thanksgiving as a family again?" he continued.

This family's reaction was typical and expected. They struggled to integrate infidelity within the family into their lives.

The aftermath of such bitterness cannot be overstated, as we saw in the Woody Allen–Mia Farrow episode that made press headlines. If Americans were stunned to find out that Allen was having an affair with the adopted sister of his children, they were shocked and revolted to learn that he eventually married her. In his movie, *Hannah and Her Sisters*, the famous film maker explored the theme of an affair in the family, portraying Hannah's husband as having an affair with Hannah's sister. An interesting aspect of this is the devastating effect it had on Hannah, even though she was unaware of its existence. (It is worth noting that in real life, by contrast, a family affair is very difficult to hide.)

Another family issue previously discussed was that of the artist N.C. Wyeth and his daughter-in-law Caroline. Author David Michaelis has reported that Wyeth's son Nat concluded that his father and his wife not only had an intimate relationship, but a physical one as well. Although the family continues to debate whether or not the mutual attraction became sexual, as Michaelis points out, they agreed that the relationship hurt Nat.

The Wyeth family, presumably because it has a reputation to uphold, has said little about the matter publicly. Therefore, the relationship did not become general knowledge until Michaelis described it in his book.

We have heard stories of sisters testifying against one another in custody suits resulting from family affairs. More than one woman has sat in our offices holding a newborn baby as she tearfully told us that her spouse was having sex with his sister-in-law or even his mother-in-law. Whether the infidelity has been between father-in-law and daughter-in-law, or the husband and his brother's wife, or any other combination, there is a profound sense of injury from the betrayal and abandonment by family figures.

The Homosexual Affair

Another reason for an affair is when a spouse leaves the marriage because he is in love with someone of his own sex. Such an affair provides an added dimension of frustration to the feelings of the injured spouse. Although the pain, rage, and sense of betrayal are similar to those of heterosexual affairs, the betrayed spouses have a special sense of helplessness. They believe they are in a losing battle, competing with a force against which they cannot win. The sense of helplessness stems from the feeling that nothing they do can influence the outcome. There is no ammunition strong enough to fight this battle.

Self-esteem takes an added blow when women feel that their femininity, and men their masculinity, is not enough to overcome their spouse's sexual orientation. For some this knowledge eventually gives way to relief because, unlike with heterosexual affairs, they can say, "It wasn't my fault." Until they reach this point, however, there is much anger and frustration at losing out to a person of the same sex as one's spouse.

The Exit Affair

Some individuals have an affair when they want to leave their marriage. There are a number of variations on this theme. Some people use the affair to get into therapy so that the therapist can make a difficult leave-taking easier by helping the betrayed spouse cope. Others use the affair to make the spouse angry enough to do the leave taking that the unfaithful one is afraid of initiating. And still others have an exit affair to have someone to lean on during the leave-taking.

We saw the exit affair in action when Karl brought Mimi to the office to help her cope with his affair. "She's very emotional," he told us. Indeed she was, but it seemed to us with good reason. Karl had told her he wanted a trial separation after twenty-six years of marriage to see whether his restlessness stemmed from their relationship or the stress he felt he was under at work.

"This is not a legal separation," he tried to assure us, "and if she calls a lawyer in, then I will fight her hard." Our experience has shown us that in a trial separation without a legal document or a mutually agreed-upon financial decision, the wife is often without funds. Exploring this further with Mimi and Karl, we discovered that Mimi had co-signed a large home equity loan to pay for some outstanding bills and furniture for a separate apartment with a tennis club and pool for Karl. We then knew that this was an exit affair. It was complicated by Mimi signing away some of her resources and assuming partial responsibility for a loan to set her husband up in a lifestyle that would let him leave the marriage. Only Mimi did not understand this yet.

All attempts to draw Karl into exploring their marriage and the affair were rebuffed with, "Just help my wife." Of course, Mimi was getting mixed messages; Karl was so solicitous, yet he was having an affair. Karl was bringing Mimi to us to help her deal with the emotional upheaval he was anticipating as he prepared for his future leave-taking.

In this chapter we have discussed many of the motivations for infidelity. Given the complexities of human nature, there is some overlap, and you may see more than one reason that applies to your situation. We hope we have provided you with an understanding of the factors that may have contributed to your spouse's infidelity. This understanding often leads to change and forgiveness. But most importantly, it can help reduce your pain.

Chapter 3

Deception and Discovery

> "I shall ignore it, so long as the world knows
> nothing of it, so long as my name is not
> disgraced."
> — ALEXY ALEXANDROVITCH TO HIS WIFE
> *ANNA KARENINA*, LEO TOLSTOY

Deception

Your spouse engaged in adultery. Then he lied to cover up. Perhaps even more than the sex itself, the deceit and dishonesty has caused you great pain. In the aftermath of the affair, you are probably wondering, "How could he lie to me over and over again?" We hope that deepening your understanding of the nature of lies will help you sort through your feelings as you arrive at a decision about your marriage.

Types of Lies

Lies come in many forms. Black lies, for example, are deliberate statements that the teller knows to be false. When our client, Phil, came in with his wife, Denise, it was just not her affair that angered him, but what he called "the bikini episode."

It seemed that Denise modeled for Phil two new bikinis she had bought for her business trip to Las Vegas. She asked Phil which one he liked better. "You look great in both, babe, but if I had to choose, I'd pick the red. It really shows off your figure."

"Now," Phil said in our office, "she made me choose a bikini she was planning to wear for her lover on her trip to Las Vegas. I didn't know that at the time, but I sure know it now. I really feel like a fool." This is an example of a black lie because of the deliberate intention to deceive.

A white lie by contrast is a statement that is not in itself false but that omits a significant part of the truth. They are usually told to avoid hurting another person's feelings and so are viewed less seriously.

Polite social lies are white lies. According to psychiatrist Dr. Charles Ford, author of *Lies, Lies, Lies*, they serve to "lubricate interpersonal relationships." Sometimes they are expressed in such an automatic manner that they don't even register in a person's awareness. When your hostess at a dinner party overcooks the vegetables and burns the roast, most people are likely to avoid being brutally honest, but at the end of the evening, pay their compliments to the chef. Polite social lies are primarily motivated by respect and concern for the feelings of others, not by a desire to deceive.

In his classification of lies, Dr. Ford includes humorous lies that amuse the listener in which any motivation to deceive is "transient and teasing." Altruistic lies are told to relieve suffering or improve another person's feelings of self-worth. Aggressive lies, by contrast, are told with the intent to hurt someone else or to gain an advantage.

Understanding another type, defensive lies, those told to protect oneself and others, may be helpful in interpreting the meaning of your spouse's dishonesty. If your mate is withholding information about the salacious details of his affair, it may be to keep you from suffering further pain. Though often told as a means of self-protection, such lies may also be motivated by compassion for the impact of the truth on the betrayed spouse.

Cyberlies

In recent years we have seen a number of affairs that began through communication on the Internet. On-line relationships make maintaining secrecy easier and provide a unique opportunity to meet a great number of people. Personal Web sites list thousands of people; chat rooms provide a chance to interact; and e-mail makes it possible to communicate in privacy. There is presently even a Web site that actively encourages married people to conduct on-line affairs.

When Josie came to see us, she was in tears over what she had done. "I nearly had sex with a guy I met on-line. Someone told me about this Web site that got people to have affairs. I thought it would be a lark to see what goes on. I sort of got caught up in it. I spent time on-line with Chuck. He lives nearby, in East County. It was only when I met him that I thought of how dangerous this could be. He could have been an ax-murderer. Now I know why they call it 'Web site.' I felt caught and about to be preyed upon. I nearly jeopardized my marriage. I'm here because I feel so very dirty from this."

Josie was joking about the ax-murderer, but in actuality a Maryland woman was murdered by a man whom she met on the Internet. Even though he gave indications that he was violent, she still chose to travel many miles to meet him. We feel that meeting people in person whom you have first met in cyberspace can be very dangerous. Psychologist Dr. Shirley Glass warns that in relationships played out in cyberspace, people often act more sexually explicit and uninhibited than they do in personal meetings. For a married person, cyberspace relationships can threaten a marriage. The need to communicate with a stranger in cyberspace in any romantic or intimate way should be a red flag that there is a problem either with the marriage, or with an individual in the marriage. Energy should go into finding out what the problem is, rather than into spending more time on the Internet.

Discovery is, of course, always a possibility. A Connecticut woman was recently accused of adultery in a divorce suit when her husband discovered the affair by snooping in her files on the family computer. Secrecy, even on-line, is not always absolute.

The anonymous nature of the Internet makes it possible for people to be less inhibited and less honest than they might be in their everyday lives. Unfortunately, when people meet on the Net, it is impossible to determine if they are, in fact, the person whom they are purporting to be. On-line it is easy to misrepresent one's appearance, marital status, or intentions. The signs that we take for granted in face-to-face meetings, body language and eye contact, give us information about people that mere words don't. Scammers, con artists, and confidence people can easily prey on those who turn to cyberspace for company rather than trying to work on resolving the problems in their marriage.

What begins as flirting, fantasizing, or even cybersex, may lead to real life off-line infidelity. We have heard firsthand stories of clients who believed that they had fallen in love after only a few weeks or months of communicating with someone they've never actually met. One woman, Georgia, told us that she had arranged to travel to a distant city to meet Maury, a man she'd only chatted with on-line. It was easy to lie to her husband, Kurt. She had only to tell him that she was going on a business trip. She told us she had a wonderful weekend with Maury, and their new sex was great. The woman had written e-mail for months, shared the problems in her marriage, and poured out her heartfelt emotions.

Georgia's husband was devastated when he found an e-mail message from her lover that she had not deleted from the computer. She agreed to come with him to couples' therapy, but her anger after what she called "years of his emotional abuse and neglect" made her determined to leave.

"I could care less about Kurt. I can't let go of Maury or my need to chat on-line with him."

She left her husband with her two children to move in with her lover, despite his pleas.

Secrets

A secret is something known by one or more persons but purposely hidden from others. Secrets are closely related to lies. Keeping an affair secret inevitably requires the infidel to lie. Sometimes a secret also involves self-deception in that the person focuses solely on the protective function of the secret and ignores its potential destructiveness.

Some couples have a covert agreement about secrets. In this kind of marriage, one spouse usually says something like, "If you do it, don't tell me about it." When she says this, it can be perceived as permission for the affair and for secrecy. "I don't want to know about his affair," one woman in our group said. "I just don't want to hear about it, and I don't want to have to do anything about it." For this woman it felt less painful to hear nothing than to learn the truth.

Ella was such a woman. "I know he's cheating on me," she told us. "It hurts so terribly. We've been married nearly twenty-eight years. I guess he wants a younger model. If I bring up the affair, I'm afraid he'll leave me, and at my age and with no skills, I'll never find a job. So, I let him lie to me."

"Do I feel powerless?" Ella went on. "You bet, but not as powerless as a minimum wage employee at age fifty-four."

"Are you angry?" we asked Ella.

"Of course. I'm outraged. It doesn't mean I am not angry because I'm going along with it."

Ella did not want to chance bringing his affair into the open, even with the possibility of having the affair end.

Gender Differences

Psychologist Dr. Dory Hollander interviewed ninety-five men and women who volunteered to talk about trust and deceit in their personal relationships. She concluded that men lie more frequently than women. For men, lies often serve as a useful tool, both in the public world of profit and business and in their private lives. Disingenuous flattery, insincere promises, and bald-faced lies are time tested strategies that men use from the boardroom to the bedroom. Men more than women use lies to achieve short-term goals, to resolve differences, or to preserve their autonomy and independence.

Monica Lewinsky, for example, testified that President Clinton told her that he "might be alone in three years," and insinuated that he might be free and available then. Ms. Lewinsky went on to say, "I left that day just sort of stunned, for I knew he was in love with me."

Men who have a need to control often lie to achieve their goals. One case, we recall, was Alfred, who was caught having an affair and decided to give it up and work on his marriage. The discovery came shortly before the holiday season.

"I'll spend Christmas with you," he told his wife, Mindy, "but I'll have to be with her for Thanksgiving. She's expecting me to celebrate with her family. I'm afraid if I break off now, her four older brothers are going to do something dangerous to you."

"Like what?" Mindy asked.

"Like slashing your tires," Alfred said.

"Bull! That's a bunch of bull, Alfred. If you don't give her up immediately, I'll slash *your* tires!"

Mindy told us that Alfred was a very controlling man, and that she had grown accustomed to his lying to get what he wanted.

"I'm not going along with it," she told him and us.

Dr. Hollander's survey found that fewer men than women agonized over the impact of their lies. Men tended to be better able to compartmentalize and to separate their lies from the emotional injury to their partners. They consistently underestimated the potential damage of their dishonesty.

In his book, *Private Lies*, psychiatrist Dr. Frank Pittman describes the masculine code of honesty. "Central to all the conventions of male honor is the sense that females are the ultimate outsider, that males must band together to protect themselves from females. . . . Truly masculine men are not supposed to need closeness to anyone, except for sex with women and games with men. Real men don't have sex with men or games with women . . . women are the sexual playing field on which men compete with one another in sexual display."

A study of dishonesty in the dating of college students found that 60 percent of the women said that they had been lied to for the purposes of obtaining sex, and 34 percent of the men admitted to having lied for that reason. Furthermore, 4 percent of the men and 42 percent of the women stated that they would understate the number of partners they previously had to a new sexual partner.

Men and women lie about different subjects. It is not uncommon, for example, for a woman to lie to make a man feel good about himself or his sexual performance. When an affair comes to light, our experience has shown that women will often blame themselves for their spouse's sexual misconduct and swallow their resentment to avoid repercussions.

Viewers of the popular *Seinfeld* television show, may remember the hilarious episode in which Jerry finds out that his former girlfriend, Elaine, "faked" orgasms when they had been lovers. Jerry is completely disturbed by this revelation. His ego took a terrible beating, and Elaine was very sorry that she hadn't kept her lie secret.

In *The Erotic Silence of the American Wife*, author Dalma Heyn conducted extensive research on the subject of infidelity. She found that many married women entered into affairs as an escape from "a culturally imposed prison" that denied them "their sexual voice." They definitely did not want to disclose their liaisons to their husbands. These nontraditional women actively sought extramarital affairs, and many expressed little or no guilt about maintaining them. As one woman stated, "I'm doing what I need to do for myself." When this insensitive and callous attitude of indifference to the betrayed spouse's feelings is expressed, as we occasionally have seen in our practices, the impact is often compounded.

The overwhelming majority of the women interviewed by Dalma Heyn believed that rather than harming their marriages, their illicit relationships reawakened their dormant sexuality and tended to improve the quality of their marriages. Instead of choosing to end their affairs, they wanted to find a way to continue them and integrate them into their marriages. Like many men, they were able to compartmentalize and wanted to maintain both their affair and their marriage. Heyn's investigation found that many women accurately believed that if their affairs were discovered, rather than reconciliation, the most likely outcome would be divorce. Consequently, they carefully guarded their secrets.

Discovery

"I'm having an affair." "There's someone else." "I saw your wife with another man." These words pierce the heart with pain and announce the discovery of an affair. And if you were not aware of the affair, the news may shock you. From the moment an affair is discovered, life seems to change in drastic and sometimes frightening ways. You may feel hostage to a range of emotions, from anger to despair, and obsessed by thoughts that seem to go on forever. Sometimes you feel that people are looking at you and that everyone knows.

Laura, a member of our support group, spoke of how she had discovered her husband's affair. "It's all falling into place now," she said. "There were signs . . . things I didn't see. I mean I did see them, but I made no connection.

"Yesterday," Laura faltered, "someone called to say that Michael was having an affair with his secretary." She paused and said, "I confronted him, and he admitted it. I didn't even think of an affair. Where was I? How could I be so dumb? I don't know how it happened. And there it was, going on right before my eyes.

"I wonder what went wrong. I thought we were working together on this fertility problem. We were supportive; we communicated. I thought I was doing everything right. How could this have happened to me?" she cried.

"I can't understand it. I mean, we had sex. Heaven knows, it was always on my mind, having sex, trying to figure out when I was fertile, trying to know when the time was right. Maybe that was it. I guess sex lost its excitement and became a chore—something to be done on schedule. Maybe he believed I was thinking of him as a sperm repository, not as a lover."

Laura continued talking this way in the group, trying to make sense of what had happened. She obsessively reviewed the events, trying hard to find the cause, and mostly trying to face what seemed to her to be unbelievable.

As therapists, we have heard countless stories like Laura's from both men and women. Our clients have shared with us their suffering after the discovery and the devastating effects of extramarital sex on their relationships.

The ways that people find out about the infidelity vary and are sometimes determined by the type of affair or the partner's plans. We have all heard about cases in which an unsuspecting spouse accidentally discovers an affair or an offending partner decides to tell. Older children often suspect and ask about it. Sometimes a friend or a neighbor delivers the news, with various motives, one of which is believing that it is in the best interest of the spouse to know the truth. But often it is the "other woman" or "other man" who ultimately informs the startled spouse about the affair.

Keeping infidelity a total secret from one's spouse requires a lot of effort. Even when it is undetected, the tension, insecurity, and deception may hurt the relationship. Extramarital sex usually leads to emotional distance and decreased attention to the marital partner. Issues within the marriage are likely to be avoided rather than dealt with, and sexual encounters between the spouses may decrease. Time and energy that might be spent with the partner become invested in the affair instead.

One woman told us that she first began to suspect her husband was having an affair because of the many hang-up phone calls she received. She decided to sign up for the "Star 69" feature with her phone company, which allowed her to dial back any incoming call. "I felt prepared," she told us, "for the next hang-up call. When it came, I 'Star 69'd' it."

The woman who answered listened to our client's story. She was very surprised to find out that her lover was a married man and the father of four kids. The other woman apologized to our client and said, "I'm going to give him hell. I don't want him. You can have him." Then she hung up.

Modern technology has given "the amateur detective" some new gadgets for her investigation. We have heard, in addition to the ever-popular "Star 69", of women who now check their spouses' calendars, whether electronic or on their computer, as well as their e-mail, for the chance of finding incriminating evidence.

As our client Max told us, "I thought I could keep Pauline from knowing about my affair. But when I look back over it, I really acted differently toward her. Things we could have done together and enjoyed I did with Bernice instead. Even though I wouldn't have left Pauline for Bernice, it drove an invisible wedge between us. Pauline felt neglected, and I wasn't even aware of it."

Max continued, "I guess it was a distraction. Pauline and I disagreed about some things, and maybe I avoided that stuff by my affair with Bernice. But Pauline never caught on. She's pretty smart. How did I put that over on her?"

Max was puzzled by Pauline's apparent obliviousness to his affair. Actually, Pauline was in denial. Denial is a defense mechanism that protects you from recognizing or acknowledging an event that is extremely painful, frightening, or reminiscent of past injuries. For example, Pauline may have been too terrified at the prospect of the breakup of her marriage to face the disturbing truth about Max's behavior.

Revealing an Affair

Some states have divorce laws that are obstacles to revealing an affair. These are states in which adultery is grounds for divorce or states that do not have community property laws. Community property laws allow for a fifty-fifty split of marital finances and possessions, excluding personal gifts and premarital property.

Where laws concerning adultery exist, unfaithful spouses are not likely to reveal an affair for fear that it will be presented in court and that the financial settlement will be unfavorable. Women who are having an affair are also afraid to reveal it for fear they will lose custody of their children. We have seen custody battles fought out of spite rather than with the child's best interest at heart.

Private investigators are often hired to sniff out an affair by those who suspect their spouses are involved with another person. This only contributes to the atmosphere of suspicion, deceit, anger, and fear. For all these reasons, the honesty and openness we think are vital to resolving the crisis are harder to establish with such laws on the books. An atmosphere of cooperation is nonexistent when one spouse is hiding an affair and the other is investigating him.

What, then, can one do to bring an affair out into the open under such circumstances? We will share with you some of the creative strategies our clients have told us. One woman, Dorelle, who lived in a state where adultery was grounds for divorce, said to her husband, "If you were having an affair, I would be very hurt. I would probably know that there was someone else because after twelve years, I know you very well. I would hope that it would end because I believe in our marriage and ability to work out our problems." Dorelle reported a change in his behavior, and later they went for marriage counseling.

Others have directly reported their suspicions to their spouses. When there was no admission of guilt, and they detected what they thought was a lie, they told the spouse to stop. This, of course, did not always stop the affair, but it was a step beyond denying feelings and suspicions.

Many spouses choose to keep their suspicions to themselves but propose marriage counseling. Jonathan, a client, told us that he was certain his wife would deny having an affair, and so he requested marriage counseling. He told his wife there were problems in their relationship and that they should work to resolve them. Eventually she told Jonathan about the affair. Although it was a fling, it was also an exit affair; that is, it was an intention to leave. Their marriage could not be saved, but they were able to bring the affair out into the open and work more cooperatively.

Should You Reveal Your Own Affair?

Most people ask themselves, "What will happen if my spouse finds out about the affair? Should I tell? Will it backfire? Or can the marriage benefit from it?" Marriage counselors who are experts on the subject are not in agreement about whether, or to what extent, an affair should be revealed.

A number of respected experts advocate total honesty. In *Private Lies*, Dr. Frank Pittman strongly advises that infidelity be revealed. He states, "In marriage retributions are cheap compared with enmity and disrespect. In marriage intimacy is developed through confessions, explanations, and soul searchings . . . The lie may be a greater betrayal of the relationship than the misdeed being lied about. It takes very little misinformation to disorient and destroy a relationship."

Emily Brown, author of *Patterns of Infidelity and Their Treatment*, agrees with Pittman. She maintains that all secrets are "crazy making."

On the other side of the issue, some therapists are of the opposite opinion. They view infidelity as not only acceptable, but sometimes even beneficial to a marriage. Our point of view, which we shall discuss in more detail shortly, is a middle-of-the-road position. Although we recommend honesty in most cases, there are situations where it may be harmful to the people involved.

In her paper, "Attractions and Affairs: Fabulous and Fatal", Dr. Florence Kaslow points out that a gulf exists between therapists who insist that the secret must always be broken and the "affairees" themselves who are uncomfortable with complete honesty. The expert's advice in regard to revealing an affair may reflect whether he or she is speaking theoretically or from direct experience with real patients seen in an office. She poses a key question that should always be considered when making a decision to disclose the affair, "Whose life is it anyway?" a perspective with which we fully concur.

Dr. Kaslow recommends considering the motivations for infidelity. She cautions that when a revelation does occur, timing is of the essence, and the most opportune moment for telling should be selected by those whose lives are most likely to be impacted. It is those who are involved who have to live with the fallout and "may or not be able to reconstruct their lives after the disclosures." This fallout may be likened to a major volcanic eruption in the sense that "it is hard to predict who the hot lava will burn before it cools down" and how those involved in the affair will be able to "sort through the ashes."

We believe that words like "always" and "never" do not apply to every situation. Such attitudes fail to take into consideration the differences between individuals and their unique circumstances. When deciding whether to reveal or not to reveal an affair, it is imperative to consider the potential short- and long-term consequences of disclosure. People may have a variety of reasons for keeping their affair secret. When people worry that they will be embarrassed, punished, or abandoned because of their affair, they will try hard to keep it secret.

Past Affairs

Many of our clients have asked us whether it is ever wise to reveal a past affair. Reasons for wanting to confess a long past liaison vary from person to person. Guilt is probably the most common motivation. By revealing his or her past transgression, promising never to cheat again, and seeking forgiveness, the infidel hopes to clear his conscience. Some people have decided to repent and disclose a long protected secret affair due to religious conviction. Others make a belated commitment to an idealistic honor code, which includes open and honest communication in marriage.

One of our clients decided to confess after keeping an affair secret for thirty years! Despite the passage of time, he still felt guilty, and he believed that by finally "getting it off his chest" he would be able to put it behind him. His confession was extremely upsetting to his elderly wife. Although it relieved him of his burden, his disclosure caused the spouse who had been kept in the dark for so long unnecessary pain.

The response to the news of a past affair is often the same as it would have been years earlier when it happened; that is, feelings of betrayal, rage, and despair. Now considerably older, the partner may have fewer options and less energy to take any action.

Disclosing an old secret rarely benefits the marriage. If you need to confess, see a spiritual or religious counselor. If there was ever a situation to which the adage "let sleeping dogs lie" applies, this is it.

A few have decided to reveal an old affair simply to hurt their spouse and "get even" for some perceived act of deceit or unfairness. Occasionally we have seen a spouse dig up the past as a way to end the marriage. If this is the underlying motivation, the same advice applies. See a marriage counselor, because there are more effective ways to handle this.

Recent Affairs

Revealing the truth about a recent affair is a complex issue. There are many costs and benefits to the marriage that need to be considered. Among the reasons that we have identified for keeping an affair secret are the following:

1. Concerns about domestic violence are the most compelling reasons for keeping an affair secret. When the betrayed spouse is

likely to "fly off the handle" and resort to physical abuse under stress, we do not advise revealing an affair. We have only to remember the O.J. Simpson case as an example of this. Even though he was not married to Nicole at the time of her murder, he was suspicious of Nicole's having an affair. All indications were that O.J. still considered her to be his.

This case shows the potential for danger when a violent man learns of or suspects an affair. If you live with such a person, it is far better for your safety and that of your children, if there are any, to see a therapist or go to a shelter. Your priority is not the affair but the problems of living with domestic violence.

2. Concerns about preserving the marriage and avoiding divorce when you believe that your spouse will never tolerate the knowledge of your infidelity.

An example of this is the man who cannot tell his wife of his affair because of her sensitivity to infidelity based upon her father's long history of philandering.

3. Concerns about the emotional effect on a fragile partner. In some situations the betrayed spouse may have a history of depression, suicide attempts, or substance abuse, and the risks of telling are likely to outweigh the benefits of honest communication.

We remember one client who expressed concerns about revealing a current affair to his wife. She took an overdose of sleeping pills three years earlier when she discovered he had had a "one-night stand."

"My memories of that night in the emergency room still haunt me," he told us.

4. Concerns about humiliation and embarrassment to the betrayed spouse. This factor is particularly relevant when the partner is a high-profile political figure or community leader, and there is a possibility that the secret might some day become public knowledge.

This reason is common. The one that stands out in our memory is the woman whose husband was a clergyman who often spoke out and wrote about the importance of family strength and unity. "I would be a real embarrassment to him if his congregation knew that I had a lover," she told us.

On the other hand, there are a number of compelling reasons to reveal the truth about infidelity that must be considered. They include the following:

1. Revealing infidelity makes it possible to find its cause and thus improve the quality of your marriage. Once the affair is out in the open, you and your spouse can explore new ways to rejuvenate the existing relationship. Besides causing great pain to the betrayed spouse, it can have a significant negative effect on children who may eventually learn the truth about their parents' "relationship." Telling the truth about an affair provides the best hope of strengthening the marriage.

    One client, Annette, told her husband, shortly after revealing her affair, "I was wrong to think an affair would solve my problems. Something is disturbing me. Even though you and the children didn't know about the affair, I could tell you were affected by it. I know we can be great together again. I want to find out what's wrong and work to make a change."

2. Revealing infidelity has personal benefits. The fear of discovery is eliminated. It clears the way to obtain professional counseling.

    Our client Brenda told us she felt enormously relieved "to have it out in the open. I agonized over it, but the preparation I did to tell him about the affair in the best manner possible helped me with this."

3. Revealing infidelity before an accidental discovery gives those involved an opportunity to end the affair and manage the situation before it can bring disgrace and humiliation to the betrayed spouse, family members, and possibly the community.

    Our client John knew his wife was becoming suspicious. "It's only a matter of time," he told us. "I'd rather tell her myself, before some neighbor does."

4. Revealing infidelity can reduce the possibility that another extra-marital affair will occur. The spouse can resume the role of confidant and ally rather than sharing secrets with a third party, which creates a triangle and weakens the marriage bond.

    Psychologists Dr. Shirley Glass and Dr. Thomas Wright tell their clients about the walls that lies and deceit build up between a couple. This wall blocks the spouse off from her partner, and instead pairs her spouse with his lover. Truth and sharing knock down the wall and open a window to the affair.

5. Revealing infidelity can alert your partner to the possibility that her health may be jeopardized by sexually transmitted diseases, which must be detected and, if present, treated.

Clues

Discovery is often not the result of being told but of finding clues that expose the affair. Clients have told us about finding motel charges on credit card receipts, long-distance or cell phone bills, love letters, and revealing entries in appointment books left lying around. Other typical clues are not leaving phone numbers in order to avoid being reached, being unavailable for ordinary family events because of sudden workload increases, attending more conferences, entertaining more clients, taking longer business trips, or other abrupt changes in habits.

Some spouses search for clues, others ignore obvious ones. Clara, a mother of two children, shared the following story. "My husband, Ron, doesn't make enough money as a teacher," she explained, "so four months ago he took a second job doing lawn work on the weekends. I don't like it because he's always outdoors, and I can't reach him by phone."

"He's really tired from the job. He's too tired to have sex. He works so hard. A friend called me last week and said she's seen Ron twice with another woman having breakfast in a restaurant in her neighborhood."

Clara sighed as she continued. "I asked him about it, and he said I was being ridiculous. He told me that he wasn't having breakfast with anybody. In fact, he was angry that I could even believe such a story when he was working so hard for us." Clara, like many others, ignored obvious signals.

Many women have told us they did not suspect an affair even after their husbands stopped wearing their wedding bands. Those who asked were often satisfied with questionable replies. One of the most common excuses we have heard was that "It isn't necessary to wear a ring to show my commitment."

This happened to our client, Brigit, a young and very attractive woman with four children. Brigit was very devoted to her husband and family, and she did not understand why Harold, her husband of ten years, would remove his wedding band. He told her that "Wearing a wedding ring isn't modern" and "Maybe you don't trust me." The result was that Brigit felt guilty about her suspicions. As it turned out, Harold was not having an affair, but he was looking for one. The wedding ring is a symbol of commitment and a "hands off" sign, meaning, "I am married." For spouses who customarily wear a wedding ring, removing it may signal availability. But when the offended partner is in denial, these obvious messages do not register.

Any radical changes in behaviors may indicate that a partner is having an affair. When we first saw Beverly in our office, it was because Roger, her conservative husband, suddenly changed. "He started working out and spends our family money on toys like a red sports car," she cried. It turned out that Roger was having an affair.

We watched something similar in the case of Lloyd, a tall, strapping policeman who was trying hard to control the anger he was feeling. He told us that he began to suspect his wife Rita of having an affair when her sexual behavior began to change. "At first, I was really happy that she was so turned on. She was much more passionate and wanted to have sex more often. It just suddenly occurred to me that she was two-timing me, and damn it, she was with another guy on the force."

Rita's sudden change in sexual behavior was the clue for Lloyd that she was having an affair.

Not every married man who buys a red sports car, or every woman with heightened sexual interest, is having an affair. But radically changed behavior is frequently an indication that a couple needs to examine their relationship.

Many unfaithful partners want to be found out, but they cannot bring themselves to broach the subject. Sometimes flaunting an affair is a way to force the hand of a spouse who refuses to acknowledge that the marriage is in trouble. Others may actually want the partner to be the one who initiates the dissolution of the marriage, thus relieving them of guilt and enabling them to tell friends and family that it "wasn't my decision."

Some may have found their affair to be unsatisfying, yet are unable to end it themselves. They may leave clues so that the spouse can find out and end it for them. Still others may have decided that the clandestine meetings and secrecy are not worth the trouble.

Sometimes the suspicious partner may become a sleuth searching for clues. Blanche, a small and very effervescent woman, was the first client we had seen who had taken on this role. She told us about her tireless efforts to catch her husband when she thought he was having an affair. Blanche could be found in her car at all hours of the day or night, watching the apartment she thought of as "their love nest." It was nothing for her to spend hours outside buildings, apartments, or theaters waiting to find the proof. Blanche carefully reviewed her husband's appointment book, and then she asked what she thought were subtle questions about his activities. Blanche never caught him, but he finally told her on his own.

Many of our clients have become detectives or hired them to find answers. Such sleuthing is very difficult to do, and hiring professionals is not only very expensive but very hard emotionally. Sometimes asking a direct question or voicing a concern about the marriage might be a more effective approach.

Confrontation

"I know he's having an affair," Dinah said. "His whole behavior has changed. I am sure it is someone at work. He whistles when he's getting dressed, and he works late a lot. I don't seem to be as important to him as I used to be."

"I see all the clues," she told the group, "but I can't seem to talk to him about it. I get this lump in my throat, and I can't talk. I guess I want to know, and yet I don't want to know."

Dinah is going through a difficult time, experienced by many people who strongly suspect an affair but are terrified to know. For some people it takes time to build the courage to ask. Time is needed to ready yourself for hearing the news in the event that your suspicions are well founded. Sorting through your feelings and the possible answers to your question is good preparation for such a confrontation. Asking a partner if he has been unfaithful is a delicate matter and may require some planning.

The likelihood of getting a truthful answer depends in part on how safe you make it for him to be honest. Certainly he knows that the truth will open the gates to an emotional response. Expressing the hurt and anger is appropriate when an affair is revealed, but if he anticipates a scene with loud recriminations and name calling, he may back off. When you reveal your suspicions, try to select an appropriate time and place and emphasize the importance of the relationship. In this setting he may feel safe enough to tell you. You, of course, must feel strong enough to hear the truth.

His truthfulness may also depend on the kind of affair he is having and the reason for it. He may be more apt to discuss his infidelity if there is not emotional attachment with the other woman, if he is feeling guilty and wants to end the affair, or if he has used the affair in order to draw attention to a problem in the marriage. If he is having a romantic love affair and has decided to leave the marriage, he might use the opportunity to inform you. A truthful answer depends on many factors.

Although many of these factors are beyond your control, you are in charge of your attitude and your behavior. You can decide what is acceptable to you, how you will act, and what it is you want. If he tells you that he is not having an affair and you are still suspicious, you have the opportunity to express your desire for a monogamous relationship. A goal to strive for is keeping the door open for his disclosure by presenting a willingness to listen and to work toward a solution.

A Volcano of Pain

Most of us begin our marriage with a sincere commitment to uphold our vows and support the basic values of loyalty, trust, and fidelity. We expect that our emotional needs for love, support, and acceptance will be met by our spouses. We place our trust in our partners and believe they will not betray us. So when infidelity occurs, it is a breach of sacred vows, and we are aware that trust in the marriage has died. Even if the infidelity has been suspected, the discovery that vows have been broken and your partner has lied gives way to an explosion of emotions, much like an erupting volcano.

When this happens, it is only human to question your self-worth. The betrayed partner may feel rejected and humiliated. At the same time, the spouse who has been involved in the infidelity may experience an increase in his or her self-esteem. By virtue of the affair, the unfaithful spouse typically feels more attractive, likable, and confident.

Jordan, a middle-aged man we had seen after his wife's affair, told us, "I thought the new hairstyle and the new way of dressing were for me. She seemed to sparkle. I thought it had to do with her new job and the confidence she was feeling from it. Well, in a way it did have to do with her work. She met a guy there that she was having an affair with. After she told me, I felt like hell. I had been fooling myself. I never thought some other guy was making her so happy. I wondered what was wrong with me that I couldn't bring out that sparkle."

A case that received national attention was that of Betty Broderick in San Diego, California. She was convicted of the double murder of her former husband, Dan, a successful and prominent attorney, and his second wife, Linda. This was an extreme example of how the violation of trust in the marital relationship can evoke intense pain and rage.

Betty Broderick had first learned that Dan was losing interest in their marriage when he told her that she was "old and fat and boring." A short time later, Betty suspected Dan of having an affair with his recently hired young legal assistant, Linda. It was only after Dan moved out of the family home that he admitted his infidelity.

The case attracted national attention for a number of reasons. One was that it involved the private lives of a wealthy, prominent couple in an affluent suburb. A second reason that seemed more significant was that it attracted the sympathy of thousands of women who were able to identify with the pain and humiliation that Betty Broderick felt. When Betty said that Linda was living *her* life, it touched a nerve in many women who had watched a husband's former lover become his new wife.

During the trial, Dr. Don-David Lusterman, a defense witness and psychologist, presented his views on the psychological effects of infidelity and its capacity to leave a betrayed spouse with an enduring sense of rage. According to Dr. Lusterman, rage can fester and grow well beyond the divorce, "unless a wandering husband admits responsibility for his wife's anguish and expresses remorse for it." He testified that "it's as if the person is an uncapped volcano of pain."

Dr. Lusterman went on to state that the underlying problem in marital affairs is the violation of trust stemming from lies told by an offending spouse while the affair continues. He further testified that "there's a tremendous sense of unreality about the jilted spouse's very being. She wonders how she could have been such a fool." Although murder is an extreme and rare reaction, intense feelings are common to all cases.

The Impact

Why does infidelity have such an enormous impact on the offended spouse? Since biblical times it has been viewed as an ethical violation. Despite today's more liberal attitudes, the majority of Americans still regard extramarital sex as the peak of disloyalty.

This was clearly shown in the polls taken after President Clinton's televised grand jury appearance and the publication of the *Starr Report*. The poll results were significant because people were able to register their disapproval of the behavior of a president whose job performance they valued.

Based on their survey of twelve thousand couples, sociologists Phillip Blumstein and Pepper Schwartz point out that even partners who have had affairs still regard monogamy as an ideal. They conclude that spouses who did *not* react to a partner's affair as a catastrophe felt that their relationship was doomed anyway.

Psychiatrist and author Dr. Aaron Beck explains that an affair has a traumatic effect on the marriage because of its symbolic meaning. Just as the bonds of marriage represent love, the symbolic meaning of infidelity is conveyed in words such as cheating, betrayal, and deceit. Infidelity is an attack on your relationship that breaches the trust between you and your spouse. After discovering an affair, your faith in your partner may be shattered. You may feel rejected, unloved, and powerless. Many of our clients have told us that being deceived caused them even more pain than the knowledge that their spouse was sexually involved with another person.

After the blow of discovery, you may find that your life becomes disorganized and chaotic. Your self-esteem is likely to suffer. You may begin to doubt your attractiveness, desirability, or worthiness. Some of our clients have experienced health problems such as stomach aches, headaches, and muscle tension. After infidelity comes to light, you will experience a wide range of emotions. In particular, you will need to deal with your pain, rage, and jealousy.

Part II

Coping and Healing

Chapter 4

Coping with the Pain

"People are disturbed not by things, but by the
views they take of them."
— EPICTETUS

"It can't be," sobbed a stunned wife in our support group. "To think he'd lie
to me over and over again! I've really been a fool. I mean nothing to him.
I feel like I've lost everything." Numbed by the pain, she looked around the
room and questioned. "Didn't he care that he'd break my heart?"

The shock this woman expressed may be similar to what you felt
when you discovered that your spouse was unfaithful. Even if you suspected infidelity, knowing for certain is intensely disturbing. Only after
emotions have subsided can you begin to look at the betrayal with more
objectivity. Although wise decisions are based on understanding the meaning of the infidelity, you cannot expect to be rational so soon after hearing
the news. This will come later.

Grief and Loss

Human beings face loss on a daily basis. We may hardly notice the small-
er ones. They do not hurt so much. But the larger, more emotional losses
take time to heal. Grief is a normal response to the trauma of loss, just as a
wound or burn is to physical trauma.

Many of our clients have found it helpful to understand and discuss
the five stages of grief identified by Dr. Elizabeth Kubler-Ross. We hope
that you will be reassured to know that the raw emotions and the ups-and-
downs that you may be suffering have also been experienced by others.
However, not everyone goes through all five stages. In fact, they are not
necessarily sequential, and sometimes people jump back and forth among
them on their way to recovery.

Stage 1: Denial

"This can't be happening to me. I must be dreaming." If you have thoughts like this, you may be experiencing denial, the first stage. It is similar to the reactions of people who have experienced other losses, including death. Your initial reaction to the discovery that your mate has been unfaithful may be disbelief. In physical injury, shock is the body's way of protecting you against the reality of hurt in case the pain becomes too great to bear. Just as the body grows numb, so can the human heart. The numbness may last for a short or long time, depending on how long you need protection against your emotional pain. You may recognize denial in your situation, or if not, you may have seen it in operation with someone you know.

Residents of the state of Maryland were once given a view of denial when they read their morning papers to see the latest developments in the lives of their governor and First Lady, Marvin and Barbara Mandel. When the governor asked his wife to leave the governor's mansion because he was in love with another woman, Mrs. Mandel refused. He moved into a motel, and she remained in the governor's mansion. Mrs. Mandel soon moved out, and they were later divorced.

As this case illustrates, eventually the actual situation is acknowledged and the denial stage ends.

Stage 2: Anger

After denial, the offended spouse is likely to experience an explosive outpouring of anger. If you are feeling rage, you can be assured it is an expected response to discovering infidelity. At this stage some people throw tantrums, and others vow revenge. The urge to retaliate may be very strong. It is at this stage that we see the woman who tosses her husband's clothes outside the house or gives his best Armani suits to the Goodwill. One woman reported that after her husband found out about her affair, he smashed her teapot collection.

One of our clients, Barbara, whose husband had been unfaithful to her, expressed her feelings at this stage by exclaiming, "I'm absolutely furious. To think he would have the nerve to carry on that way right under my nose. The louse! I could kill him." She sobbed, "After the pain he's caused me, I want him to suffer too."

When you are able to acknowledge your anger and express it in a safe way, you are on your way to working through your grief. In the following chapter, we will discuss this stage in more depth and provide you with some tools to handle this powerful emotion.

Stage 3: Bargaining

When the anger dissipates, the bargaining stage begins. Beginning to face the fact that your marriage is in a crisis, you may start bargaining. "I promise to be more considerate." "I'll be more loving." "I'll try to be better in bed." "I'll change my ways and be more attentive." In the bargaining stage, you may be so hurt and terrified of losing the relationship that you are not able to think rationally.

Betty Jean, a faithful member of our support group on infidelity, told us how she wanted to impress her husband with her devotion, and she did so by ironing his shirts when he went on dates. Members of the group were angry with her. They correctly saw this behavior as supporting his infidelity and not standing up for herself. Betty Jean replied to their challenge by saying that he soon would realize what a fine wife and capable person she was to rise above the situation. Her husband left anyway.

Harvey told a similar story in his support group. Harvey was a criminal lawyer who relied on his logical skills to prepare his cases. Yet he told the group that he stayed home with the kids so that his wife could go to the theater and ballet with her lover. He went along with his wife's belief that she needed to get more out of life, since she was so young when they married. He reasoned that she would soon see who the better man was. But Harvey was mistaken; she didn't.

Stage 4: Depression

The fourth stage is depression. Tears may flow. You may feel lethargic and lose interest in the outside world. Your appetite may dwindle, or you may find yourself eating uncontrollably. Concentration may be difficult. You may become forgetful or confused.

"I was so depressed, I couldn't seem to get going," recalled one of our clients who was reacting to her husband's affair. "At first I only went through the motions, doing what I absolutely had to. I was frozen, immobilized." Another client said, "I know it's foolish to cry so much, but I can't stop. Nothing seems worth living for anymore."

Once you are depressed you may actually become your own worst enemy. For example, Princess Diana expressed her pain over her husband's infidelity through her suicide attempts, bulimia, and her extramarital affairs. Instead of caring for yourself, you may neglect yourself or your appearance. Instead of seeking pleasure, you may actually avoid it. We have heard our clients say things like, "If only I'd been more sexually responsive, he might not have strayed." "How could I have been such a blind fool?" You may falsely believe that you're being punished or that you actually deserve what happened. If you are experiencing similar thoughts or physical symptoms such as sleeplessness, loss of appetite, or inability to concentrate, medication prescribed by a psychiatrist may minimize your suffering and enable you to recover more quickly.

After discovering the affair, you can expect to experience sad feelings as important anniversary dates approach. Many women have come to our office concerned about the sadness they were feeling when they had felt they were moving forward and making progress in their recovery. In talking with them, we often found that this sadness was due to the approach of a birthday, a wedding anniversary, or the date of the discovery of the affair.

So if you feel what you think is unexplained sadness, it is possible that there is a significant anniversary approaching. This in itself helps you, because understanding the cause of your feelings is often therapeutic. However, you can often do more for yourself by planning activities you enjoy and rallying your support system to your aid.

Stage 5: Acceptance

The final stage, acceptance, is necessary for moving forward. There are two kinds of acceptance: intellectual, which comes earlier, and emotional, which comes later. Intellectual acceptance means understanding what has happened. Emotional acceptance means being able to discuss your spouse's infidelity without the intense reaction you experienced earlier.

You must remember that acceptance is the final stage of grieving. If you are at the earlier stages, this last stage may seem like an impossibility. We have heard many clients say, "I can never accept what happened." Condoning infidelity is not the same as acceptance. Acceptance simply means you have acknowledged that infidelity has occurred. The trade-off for nonacceptance is bitterness and an inability to trust again. In our experience, after enough time passes, most people are able to integrate both the emotional and intellectual acceptance of their loss.

If you have only recently discovered that your spouse has been unfaithful, understanding the stages of grief and loss will not alone be enough to end your suffering. You should be aware that the grief process may vary in time with different people, from a very short duration to a very protracted length of time. As much as infidelity seems like a death, it is a death of the hopes you had had when you were first married. It is not necessarily the death of the marriage itself. You may be able to rebuild and create new dreams.

Expressing Sad Feelings

You may wake up crying or go to sleep crying. Perhaps you will find yourself choking up unexpectedly. A sad song on the radio may trigger your tears. This phase is part of the healing process.

In our culture many people believe that emotional pain, unlike physical pain, is unacceptable. The shedder of tears is likely to apologize or to feel embarrassed. The observer of tears is likely to feel uncomfortable and try to put an end to the display. This attitude is reinforced by the media. We are shown patrons of long-distance telephone service on happy occasions, for instance, but we are not shown those who reach across the miles to provide love and support in times of crisis.

Expressing your sad feelings is healthy. Research conducted at the University of Minnesota found that emotional tears may actually play a direct role in alleviating stress. Studies of men and women who kept "crying diaries" for a month found that 85 percent of the women and 73 percent of the men said they felt better after crying. On average, the participants reported a 40 percent reduction in stress after crying.

The cultural message to suppress feelings and operate solely by reason falls heaviest upon men. The researchers found that men cry only one-fifth as often as women. They suggested that the holding back of tears may be a reason that men develop more stress-related illnesses than women do.

When you are reacting emotionally to the crisis in your marriage, it is important to turn to others. Try to spend time with your friends, your children, or with a therapist. There's something comforting about not being alone in your grief. At this stage, what you need most is just someone who can sit there with you in your pain and listen.

Obsessing

After infidelity has occurred, many of our clients have told us that they couldn't stop thinking about what happened. You, too, may find yourself mentally going over and over events that pertain to the affair or other details of your relationship. Psychiatrist Robert Weiss calls this "constant, absorbing, sometimes maddening preoccupation that refuses to accept any conclusion" an "obsessive review." We want to reassure you that not being able to get what happened out of your mind doesn't mean you are going crazy. The process may help you get an accounting of the events that have occurred and make them part of your personal history. In most cases, the obsessive thoughts and images return less and less frequently, and they cease to be a problem.

One of our clients described this preoccupation with the details pertaining to his wife's affair. "I keep going over the conversation the night she told me of the affair. It was with my partner. I can see her now, flirting with him and my not realizing what was going on. I can't get it out of my mind. I can't stop thinking about it."

In our work with clients, whether they are dealing with infidelity, separation and divorce, or some other life trauma, we have often observed this obsessive review. After the assassination of President John F. Kennedy, the constant watching of the tragic events on TV helped the nation come to terms with the tragedy and accept it as part of its history. In recent years this obsessive review was also seen in the reaction of the British people, and indeed much of the rest of the world, to Princess Diana's tragic death.

Although obsessing is a normal reaction to trauma and part of the recovery process, there are some pitfalls associated with it. One danger is that you may become stuck in the process. A second concern is that you can become obsessive about the sexual scenes between your spouse and the other person. Staying with these sexual images is not helpful and will keep you from resolving the basic marital issues.

Author and therapist Emily Brown has identified some common obsessive themes. Included are rage that someone else is reaping the rewards of your efforts; primitive feelings of jealousy or abandonment; a sense of being violated, victimized, or punished; and pain at feeling rejected and powerless.

We want to share with you a technique called "thought stopping," which can help get rid of your obsessions. The technique is simple. Shut your eyes and interrupt your intrusive thoughts or images by saying "stop" to yourself subvocally. You can also imagine a very large stop sign and think the word "stop." Some of our clients prefer to picture a series of neon lights spelling out "stop." Others find expletives such as "Go to Hell," "Shut up," or "Get out of my head" more effective than "stop."

If these strategies are not successful, you can try wearing a rubber band unobtrusively around your wrist. When unwanted thoughts occur, snap it. Finally, you might try pressing your finger nails into the palms of your hand to stop obsessive thoughts.

Another strategy is to confine your obsession by assigning a definite period for thinking about it, perhaps a half hour in the morning and in the evening. One client told us that she splashed cold water on her face when she became obsessive; another distracted himself by counting backwards from one hundred by twos or remembering all the lyrics to the score of *Hair*. The idea is to contain the obsession and to stop it.

You should be aware that even these techniques take time. Obsessive thoughts are likely to return, and you will have to interrupt them repeatedly. The main effort is to stifle each intrusive thought as it begins and to concentrate on something else. The unwelcome thoughts will return less and less frequently in most cases, and eventually they will cease to be a problem for you.

You Feel What You Think

"My husband cheated on me. Our marriage is doomed." "I'm such a loser. My wife only stays with me because I support her financially." "My husband had an affair because I wasn't good enough in bed."

These thoughts are from people who have started to view themselves and the world in a negative way. This happens when you are upset. You misinterpret events and distort them in order to fit your pessimistic outlook. It's as if you're looking at the world through a mental filter that focuses on the negative and screens out your positive thoughts. This negative mental filter may begin to color the way you think about what happens to you.

Most people do not fully appreciate the effect that thoughts have on their feelings and behavior. What you think actually determines how you feel. By falsely believing that you have been rejected, for example, you may actually make your pain worse. If you believe that you're a "failure," this negative view of yourself will contribute significantly to your feeling upset.

After you have discovered infidelity and reacted intensely, continuing your negative thinking will prolong your suffering. One of our clients, Doug, told us, "Nothing seems to be worth living for anymore. I've lost my wife's love." He was engaging in negative self-talk that caused him to feel hopeless.

The cognitive approach to coping with emotional upsets emphasizes that the real cause of your pain is not so much the external event, such as the affair, but rather the way in which you view yourself, your marriage, and your future. This approach is based on the following principle: How you *interpret* or evaluate your situation determines your emotional reaction.

In other words, even if you have good reason to feel sad about what happened, you may still be making yourself feel worse by your "self-talk." According to psychologist Dr. Albert Ellis, this happens when you "awfulize," "terriblize," and "catastrophize" about the potential consequences of your spouse's behavior. Human beings seem to have a tendency to think about the worst possible thing that could happen and then assume it inevitably will, when in reality it is only a possibility. Just because your spouse has been unfaithful doesn't necessarily mean that your relationship or future is doomed.

The ABC's of Emotion

To help you better understand the cognitive approach, we will use Dr. Ellis's model to illustrate the important relationship between your thoughts and your emotions.

A	B	C
Activating Event	Beliefs	Emotional Consequences
Your spouse has an affair.	"This is awful." "No one will ever love me again."	depressed hopeless terrified

Most people believe it is the situation (A) that causes them to feel certain emotional consequences (C). It is not, however, really (A) that causes (C). Rather, it is (B), your beliefs or thoughts about (A), that determines (C).

A	B	C
Activating Event	Beliefs	Emotional Consequences
Your spouse has an affair.	"This is highly upsetting. Our marriage needs work."	sad worried angry

In the second example, the situation (A) is the same. The emotional consequences (C), however, are quite different. The difference results from the more logical, realistic thoughts or beliefs at point (B), which are, "This is highly upsetting. Our marriage needs work."

It is understandable to feel sad, worried, and angry after you have discovered your partner's affair. From the example, you can see that the way in which you interpret the situation will affect how you feel.

Challenge Your Negative Thoughts

An important tool to help relieve your suffering is to identify your negative thoughts. Changing your thoughts can make you feel better. Ask yourself what sentences you are saying to yourself that are contributing to your upset feelings. Start looking for these sentences. Often they take such forms as "Isn't it terrible that . . ." or "Wouldn't it be awful if . . . ?" Then ask yourself, "How is it terrible that?" or "Why would it be awful if?" Begin to question and challenge your negative thoughts.

For example, instead of saying to yourself, "The fact that my wife had an affair proves that our marriage has failed," try substituting a thought like, "the fact that my wife had an affair shows that we have to solve the problems in our relationship." Listen to yourself think. Then begin substituting more realistic replacement thoughts for your negative and illogical ones.

This approach is not merely positive thinking. The difference is that simple positive thoughts may not be true, and you couldn't possibly convince yourself to believe them. Instead, our intention is to encourage you to view your spouse's actions, potential consequences of the infidelity, and your options in a more *realistic* fashion.

Themes of Negative Thoughts

Your negative thoughts may contain themes, many of which have been identified by Dr. Aaron Beck, the founder of cognitive therapy. You can reduce your pain by learning to recognize and understand why these themes are inaccurate.

1. Negative Opinion of Yourself. This theme is often brought about by comparing yourself with others who may seem to you to be more attractive or more capable. "She's got a better body than I have." "He's a better lover than I am." You may find that you have become preoccupied with these thoughts about yourself. They are likely to be based on the fact that you are feeling particularly down on yourself.

2. Self-Blame. When you are hurt and feeling blue, you may focus your attention on your perceived inadequacies. You may blame yourself for not fulfilling your role as a wife or husband as well as you think you should, for not being sexy or loving enough. You may go so far as to falsely decide that the infidelity was *entirely* your fault.

3. Negative Interpretation of Events. Over and over, you may find yourself responding in negative ways to situations that don't

usually upset you. If you misplace something, you may think, "Everything in my life is going wrong." If someone looks at you, you may think, "They're staring at me. They know what's happened." When you are dealing with a crisis like the discovery of infidelity in your marriage, it's easy to read disapproval into comments that other people make, even if they weren't intended. Of course, it is important to resist doing this.

4. Negative Expectations of the Future. It is common to believe that your misery will last forever. Perhaps you think that unhappiness is going to be inevitable. You may actually believe that you will never find love again or that repairing your relationship is impossible.

These typical negative thoughts are not usually arrived at on the basis of reason and logic. They just pop into your mind. If you examine them carefully, you will find that they are not really valid, although they may seem perfectly plausible to you at the time that you think them. Negative thinking will make you feel worse than you already do. It will also interfere with your making objective decisions about what you want for your future.

If you have only recently discovered that your spouse has been unfaithful, it is natural to feel hurt and angry. This is healthy and appropriate. The problem with negative thinking is that, in addition to keeping you stuck in your pain, it can actually aggravate your emotional state.

Negative thoughts are characterized by various distortions that lead you to believe them, despite evidence to the contrary. Dr. David Burns, author and psychiatrist, has described ten of these thinking distortions. We suggest you study the list carefully and see which of them apply to you.

Thinking Distortions

1. All-Or-Nothing Thinking. This distortion refers to your tendency to see things in an extreme way, with no middle ground. Events are put in black and white categories; there are no shades of gray. People and situations are perceived as either good or bad, winners or losers.

   You may view your spouse as either loving you or hating you, and you may rule out any possibility in between. A single one-night-stand may be enough for you to brand your partner a "liar" and a "philanderer." You perceive yourself or your marriage as a total failure.

2. Overgeneralization. You make a broad, general statement that emphasizes the negative. By using words such as "always" or "never," you may turn a single event into a catastrophe. You may think, "If my wife lied to me, she can never be trusted again." "My marriage can never be repaired." "We will never be close again."

3. Mental Filter. This distortion involves focusing on one single negative element of a situation to the exclusion of anything positive. Your selective recall of events is likely to leave you feeling more depressed or angry. This distortion can keep you from seeing or remembering the rewarding aspects of your marriage. All you recall is the pain. It is helpful to think about the good times you shared or that your husband might be a kind father and hardworking provider, not just a "womanizer."

4. Disqualifying the Positive. You ignore positive experiences because you think they "don't count." Instead, you view people or events pessimistically. You don't enjoy good feelings because you expect "the other shoe to fall." For example, you take a pleasant walk with your spouse, but all evening you are thinking, "This is great, but it won't last. Before the evening is over, we'll start arguing about the affair."

   You have recently learned that your husband had a fling. Although he has been caring, attentive, and supportive throughout your marriage, you can't think of a single, positive act on his part. When he swears he loves you, you insist that he doesn't give a damn about you.

5. Mind Reading. You assume someone is responding negatively to you without checking it out. You erroneously attribute negative motives to your partner or believe you know what he is thinking. When your spouse strokes your hair and tells you how lovely it is, you begin to think, "Oh yeah, it's probably nothing compared to hers." "My wife no longer finds me attractive. That's why she got involved with another man." Mind readers draw conclusions without testing them out. Sometimes, of course, you will be correct in your reading. It is more productive, however, if you check out the accuracy of your assumptions.

   "Fortune Telling" is a closely related thinking error. In this distortion you predict that things will turn out badly. If you are upset, you may tell yourself, "I'll never fall in love again." You may predict that it is impossible to repair your marriage before you make the effort.

6. Magnification/Minimization. This distortion refers to the tendency to magnify your mistakes and minimize your successes. If you make an error, you blow its importance out of proportion. This process has been called "catastrophizing." Catastrophic thoughts often start with the words "What if." "What if my husband leaves me? I will end up on welfare." "What if she goes off with him? Then I'll never find another love."

7. Emotional Reasoning. Essentially you think, "I feel it, therefore it must be true." If you feel unattractive, you believe it must be true. "I feel powerless. Therefore my problems cannot be solved." "I feel inadequate. Therefore, I must be a loser." The problem with emotional reasoning is that emotions by themselves may not be valid. They are determined by your thoughts.

8. Should Statements. In this distortion, you maintain a list of rules about how you and other people should behave. Statements such as "I shouldn't still be crying" or "I should be more understanding" are examples. Operating from a list of rigid beliefs, such as should statements, is likely to lead to guilty feelings, since you are not living up to your own self-imposed expectations. A betrayed wife, for example, may "should herself" with "I should have been a more attentive wife; then he wouldn't have cheated."

When you direct should statements toward others, you end up feeling frustrated and angry. You unrealistically demand that others *should* be different from the way they are. "She shouldn't have been so thoughtless." Restating these "shoulds" and "oughts" in terms of "I would prefer that . . ." "It would be nice if . . ." is more realistic.

9. Labeling and Mislabeling. Instead of accurately thinking that he had an affair and you need to understand the reasons, you label him a "philanderer" and yourself a "failure." When you engage in this distortion, you view the person's character as a problem instead of focusing on his unacceptable behavior, which, of course, he can choose to change. By labeling your spouse in this way, you do not allow for the possibility of improving the situation. An additional problem of labels is they tend to emphasize negative characteristics and ignore positive ones.

10. Personalization. This distortion occurs when you relate an event to yourself which is not entirely under your control. It refers to the tendency to see yourself as responsible for someone else's problem.

   We frequently find that men and women believe that their spouses' affair was their fault or a reflection of some shortcoming on their part. "If I had only watched him more closely, I could have prevented the affair," is an example of this thinking error. This reasoning is faulty, since what your partner chooses to do is his responsibility. Personalization often leads to feeling guilty. We want you to understand that feeling guilty doesn't mean you are guilty.

The Daily Thought Record

The cognitive approach to coping with emotional pain is an active one. Keeping a daily thought record is the most effective way to "catch" your negative thoughts. By writing them down and examining them, you can begin to determine how realistic they are. Keeping a daily record will help you become more aware of the thoughts or images that precede your unpleasant feelings. Substituting more realistic thoughts can make you feel better.

Dr. Aaron Beck* recommends you record five elements:

1. Situation. First write a brief description of the actual event that led to your feeling upset. Describe what you were doing or thinking about when you started to feel sad or angry. When you identify the upsetting event, try to be specific. For example, you might write, "My husband called and said he would be working late. He said he wouldn't be home in time for dinner."
2. Feelings. Write down the emotions you experienced. Use words like sad, guilty, hurt, anxious, etc. Next rate how upset you were on a scale from 0 to 100. Zero represents feeling calm and at peace. A score of 100 represents feeling terrible, the worst feelings you have felt. You might want to write down several feelings, because you are likely to have more than one.
3. Negative Thoughts. What was going through your mind immediately before you started to feel bad? Tune in to your "self-talk." Ask, "What am I saying to myself?" Write down the thoughts that

---

* From *Love is Never Enough,* by Dr. Aaron T. Beck. HarperCollins Publishers. Used by permission.

you associate with feeling upset. For example, when you received the phone call from your husband, you might have told yourself, "Ever since he lied to me, I haven't been able to trust him. He's probably lying to me again." You may recognize the thinking distortions of overgeneralization and mind reading in this example.

We realize that a wife might be suspicious when her husband who has been unfaithful calls to say he has to work late. It is, however, her *interpretation* rather than the actual event itself that determines her feelings. Depending on the meaning she assigns to the situation, the wife might experience many different emotions. For example, another wife, after receiving reassurances that her husband was being truthful, might be relieved that he called to assure her of his whereabouts. She could interpret the same information differently by saying to herself, "Now I will have more time to myself this evening."

4. Realistic Thoughts. How can you answer the negative thoughts realistically? After you have written them down, try to identify the distortions in them. Examine the evidence. Try to find alternative explanations. Is there anything you can do to check out the accuracy of your thoughts? For example, think back over the past to the fact that your husband mentioned that he has a deadline to meet on completing his current work project. (Of course there are some cases where distrust is justified.)

5. Outcome. How do you feel now that you have identified your negative thoughts and replaced them with more realistic "counter thoughts"? After you've developed the new thoughts, again rate how you feel. The purpose of rerating your feelings with numbers is to break the habit of thinking about emotions in an all-or-nothing manner. Successfully challenging your negative thoughts can help you feel better.

To help you understand how this method works, on the following page we have included a completed thought record. On the next page, following the sample, there is a blank record form for you to photocopy and fill in for yourself. We strongly recommend that you write down your thoughts and replace them with more realistic counter-thoughts. You will be surprised how much better you will begin to feel afterward.

The discovery of infidelity may be more wounding to your sense of self than anything you have previously experienced. We hope that the information we have shared about grief and loss and the cognitive approach to overcoming pain will help you begin to restore your self-respect and move toward your personal recovery. Of course, for your wounds to fully heal, you will want to share your feelings with your spouse and resolve your marital crisis.

Before we help you with your rage and jealousy, some reflections about life made by Virginia Satir, celebrated innovator in the field of family therapy, may comfort you. Just before her death she wrote:

> Life is not the way it's supposed to be. It is the way it is. The way you cope with it is what makes the difference . . . I think that if I have one message, one thing before I die that most of the world would know, it would be that the event does not determine how to respond to the event, that is purely a personal matter. The way in which we respond will direct and influence the event more than the event itself.

Thought Record

SITUATION What were you doing or thinking about when you started to be upset?	**RESPONSE** I spoke on the phone with my husband. He told me that he would be working late, and he wouldn't be home for dinner.
FEELINGS What emotions did you feel? Rate them on a scale from 0 (fine) to 100 (terrible).	**RESPONSE** I felt sad (80) and also angry (60).
NEGATIVE THOUGHTS What was going through your mind immediately before you felt upset?	**RESPONSE** Ever since Tom lied to me, I haven't trusted him. He's probably lying again.
REALISTIC THOUGHTS Write a realistic and constructive response to your negative thoughts.	**RESPONSE** Tom probably did have to work late. There's no evidence that he's lying. Just because I think something doesn't make it true.
OUTCOME How do you feel now that you have answered your negative thoughts? (Rerate)	**RESPONSE** I feel sad (60) and also angry (40).

Thought Record

SITUATION What were you doing or thinking about when you started to be upset?	RESPONSE
FEELINGS What emotions did you feel? Rate them on a scale from 0 (fine) to 100 (terrible).	RESPONSE
NEGATIVE THOUGHTS What was going through your mind immediately before you felt upset?	RESPONSE
REALISTIC THOUGHTS Write a realistic and constructive response to your negative thoughts.	RESPONSE
OUTCOME How do you feel now that you have answered your negative thoughts? (Rerate)	RESPONSE

Chapter 5
Handling the Rage and Jealousy

"Yet she must die, else she'll betray more men.
Put out the light, and then put out the light. . . ."
— *OTHELLO*

When someone you count on for love and support deceives you, it is natural to feel outraged. Anger is a healthy, normal response to emotional injury. Of all the emotions, however, anger is by far the most difficult for people to deal with.

We commonly see two extremes in the way people cope with anger. The first extreme is to "stuff it," that is, not to acknowledge or express it. Unfortunately, denying or attempting to disguise your anger requires a tremendous expenditure of psychic energy—energy that is better spent otherwise.

The second extreme is to overreact, that is, to rant, rave, and express unrestrained anger. Such a response is likely to make matters worse. We have heard stories of one spouse who took her husband's clothes to the dump, another tore up his wife's dissertation in progress, and still another slashed his wife's waterbed.

Acting out your vindictive urges is clearly not in your best interests and is likely to create new problems. If you want to repair your relationship, resisting the urge to retaliate is essential.

Much of the problem in handling anger lies in your associations with it. The messages you received as a child may still determine the meaning of anger for you. For example, you may have been taught that "children should be seen and not heard" or warned, "Don't you dare raise your voice to me." Perhaps you were harshly punished for "talking back" or even for displaying subtle nonverbal gestures of annoyance or irritation.

One woman reported that she was told "wipe that ugly look off your face" when her mother detected that she felt resentful. Another who smiled inappropriately whenever she discussed her lobbyist husband's affair told us that her parents never openly expressed anger in front of her when she was growing up. If you grew up with childhood messages like these, we want to help you *relearn* that anger is a normal human emotion. What you do with it makes the difference.

Women's Anger

We have observed that many women find it particularly difficult to cope with angry feelings. Dr. Harriet Lerner, author and psychologist, has explained some of the reasons for this. Women have traditionally been taught that sugar and spice are the ingredients from which they are made, and they have been expected to be society's nurturers, soothers, and peace-makers. Taboos against women expressing anger are sometimes so powerful that even being aware of your anger may not be a simple matter.

Our society often disapproves of women who openly express anger at men. Such a woman is likely to be viewed as irrational or labeled an "angry woman." She may be stereotyped with a battery of negative labels such as "bitch," "nag," "fishwife," or "shrew."

Failure to express legitimate anger is "de-selfing" writes Dr. Lerner. What does she mean by "de-selfing?" It occurs when too much of one's self (including feelings, wants, thoughts, opinions) are compromised under pressures from the relationship. A betrayed wife, for example, may ask, "What's wrong with me? Aren't I sexy enough?" rather than asking a more appropriate question such as "What's wrong with the relationship?"

Many women believe that anger is a destructive force and fear its potential consequences, which may include disapproval, rejection, and violence. In fact, we have so often heard our clients use the expression "Don't make waves" that for some women it appears to serve as a credo. If you are convinced that you cannot survive without your husband or that your self-worth and identity are to be found only in a relationship, you may hesitate to express legitimate anger. Instead, you may attempt to preserve your marriage at your own expense.

Men's Anger

Problems in dealing with anger are not just a women's issue. Many men also have difficulty dealing effectively with this powerful emotion. In their struggle to handle their rage at being "cuckolded," blame may be directed toward their rival. One husband who discovered that his wife had been having an affair described his reaction in the following way: "I felt enraged, betrayed; I felt that there was some guy out there who knew all about me and who had beaten me. Even though I didn't know who he was, he had won. I wanted to kill him."

When extramarital sex occurs, many men respond violently. Sexual jealousy is frequently cited as a motive in wife battering as well as in homicide. Typically this reaction has its roots in early experiences with a parent who knew no other way to deal with anger than to explode. If a little boy's early experience of anger is to witness his father ranting and raving, or being physically abusive, as an adult he will most likely have trouble managing his own anger.

As we discussed earlier, the way anger was dealt with in your family of origin often becomes a model for your own style of handling it. If you recognize one of these styles as yours, you probably realize that handling anger inappropriately has been a problem in the past. A key to resolving the issues connected with infidelity is understanding the nature of anger and learning to express it effectively.

Understanding Anger

Before you can fully acknowledge your anger, let alone express it constructively, you may find it helpful to learn more about it. In her well-researched book on the subject, psychologist Dr. Carol Tavris dispels some common myths about the causes and methods for dealing with anger.

Myth 1: Depression Is Always Anger Turned Inward

One myth shared by many therapists as well as lay people is that depression is really anger turned inward. Sometimes depression may be "anger turned inward." Other times, you may simply be feeling sad and miserable, as, for example, when your spouse has been unfaithful. Sometimes depression follows anger; other times it precedes it. Most often anger and depression are experienced at the same time.

When you are depressed, you may express hostility toward your unfaithful spouse, the person who caused you pain, or you may express it toward the third party. Many times people vacillate between anger and sadness.

Myth 2: Talking Out Anger Gets Rid of It

Sometimes talking out your anger doesn't reduce it. In fact, you actually run the risk of it becoming obsessive. Research studies have shown that when you recite your grievances, your emotional arousal builds up again.

As a result you may end up feeling as upset as you did when the affair was first discovered. Anger may also be "socially created." For example, if you discuss the infidelity with your friends, they may encourage you to vent your fury when actually you may be feeling more hurt than angry.

In discussing this research, Dr. Tavris points out that these findings are not intended to convince you to suppress your anger but rather to help you understand what happens when you decide to express it.

Each person must find a middle ground between expressing anger too vigorously and passively accepting betrayal, deceit, or other injustices. Being able to discuss your feelings assertively with your spouse can lead to practical solutions.

Myth 3: It Helps to Blow Off Steam

Although there is widespread belief that "getting it out of your system" is beneficial, research on this issue suggests that people who give vent to their rage actually get *angrier* rather than less angry. When you drain off pent up anger by shouting, throwing things, or verbal abuse, you may actually stimulate yourself to even stronger aggression.

This contemporary "ventilationist view," as Dr. Tavris points out, overlooks the consequences of your unbridled rage. Although shouting to your unfaithful spouse that he is a "son-of-a-bitch" might reduce your tension momentarily, it is also likely to aggravate him and cause him to retaliate. Accusations make your partner defensive. So rather than listening to you, his energies will go into defending himself, maybe shouting over you, or simply waiting for his chance to talk without hearing you. Keeping your goals in mind is what is important at this time. If your goals are to inform your partner how upset you are, to inspire him to make amends, and to change his behavior, then yelling at him might not get the desired results.

Once you have acknowledged your anger, the decision about when, where, how, or even whether you should express it is related to your goals. You must decide how you want to use your anger. We suggest that it be used as the fuel for problem solving rather than for retaliation. The important question to ask yourself is, "How can I express my anger to best accomplish my goals?"

Calming Yourself

Before you can productively deal with your rage, we suggest you begin by calming yourself. The conventional wisdom that you should count to ten before expressing your anger is actually sound advice. Another suggestion,

"Sleep on it," is also worth considering. Distraction techniques such as baking, sewing, listening to music, or going to the movies may also be helpful. Noncompetitive exercise such as walking, jogging, or aerobics is another useful means of reducing your tension.

Developing some routines that are calming prior to retiring may help you reduce your emotional arousal. These include a warm bath, a glass of tea, listening to soothing music, visualizing pleasant scenes, or meditating. Spending a few minutes planning an enjoyable activity for the next day is often relaxing.

Deep Breathing

Most people are not aware that deep diaphragmatic breathing makes use of a natural relaxation response. This response occurs when you exhale. When you exhale your muscles will generally release and relax.

A procedure for deep breathing suggested by psychologist Dr. George Everly is as follows:

Step 1: Assume a comfortable position. Place your left hand on top of your navel. Now place your right hand so that it comfortably rests on your left. Keep your eyes open.

Step 2: Imagine a hollow bottle or pouch lying internally beneath the point at which your hands are resting. Begin to inhale. As you inhale, imagine that the air is entering through your nose and descending to fill that internal pouch. Your hands will rise as you fill the pouch with air. As you continue to inhale, imagine the pouch being filled to the top. Your rib cage and upper chest will continue the wave-like rise that was begun at your navel. The total length of your inhalation should be three seconds for the first week or so, lengthening to four or five seconds as you master the procedure.

Step 3: Hold your breath. Keep the air inside the pouch. Repeat to yourself the phrase, "my body is calm."

Step 4: Slowly begin to exhale—to empty the pouch. As you do, repeat to yourself the phrase "my body is quiet." As you exhale, you will feel your raised abdomen and chest recede.

Repeat this four-step exercise four to five times in succession. Should you begin to feel lightheaded, stop. Practice this exercise to reduce your emotional arousal several times a day, if possible. Make it a ritual in the morning, afternoon, and evening, as well as when you are feeling particularly upset. Regular, consistent practice of deep diaphragmatic breathing will help you relax.

Meditation

This is another means of calming yourself. Meditation has been an important component of the world's major religious traditions for thousands of years. It can help you reduce your emotional arousal, express your anger constructively, and create a sense of peace and tranquillity.

In meditation, the purpose is to "flow with" or "be with" the experience. Think of the times you have found yourself totally absorbed in listening to a beautiful piece of music or receiving a massage. At that time, you were unlikely either to analyze your experience or to attempt to control it. This sort of mental posture is very similar to that required in meditation.

When we discussed obsessing in the previous chapter, we pointed out that it is difficult to stop thinking about the details of the affair. The ability to turn off obsessions and focus on something else is an important aid in calming yourself. In meditation, your attention is focused on a single object, such as a word, a phrase, a sound, a sensation of the breath or body, or a visual object.

A procedure for meditation is as follows:

> Try to get as comfortable as possible. Close your eyes and allow your breathing to become natural and relaxed. Soon it will reach its own rhythm and depth. Now concentrate on your breathing. Focus your entire attention on it. When you do this, thoughts and sounds will no longer disturb you.
>
> To further focus your attention on your breathing, try thinking two words to yourself. The words are *in* and *out*. As you slowly inhale, think the word *in*; as you slowly exhale, think the word *out*. Practicing meditation regularly will help you calm yourself.

Visualization

This is a useful technique for handling catastrophic, repetitious, negative thoughts or images. It consists of imagining a calm scene. The scene is to be a snapshot picture that includes specific details of what you see, hear, smell, and sense. You might imagine yourself lying on the beach listening to the sound of waves and feeling a cool breeze blowing across your face, or walking in the woods with sun warmly shining on you while birds sing in the trees.

The calm scene may be a particularly relaxing situation you enjoyed in the past, or it may be an ongoing situation—taking a bubble bath, sitting in an armchair listening to music, or some other personally relaxing experience.

A procedure for visualization is as follows:

> Prepare to relax by breathing deeply and evenly. Breathe in slowly to a count of four. Hold your breath to a count of four; exhale slowly. As you continue to breathe deeply and evenly, imagine your calm scene in vivid detail as if it were happening now. Remember the sights, the smells, the feelings, and the mood. Just let yourself relive the moments. Breathe deeply and evenly as you relax and enjoy the memory. Repeat this procedure until you feel calm.

Just Because

Dr. Ellen Quick developed an "instant" technique that you may find useful. It is called, "Just Because," and it includes a sentence you say to yourself. Take a deep breath and think, "Just because . . . (insert whatever is troubling you; for example, my partner was unfaithful) . . . doesn't mean I have to do this to my body. Now RELAX . . ." and make "RELAX" your cue to exhale. Take a deep breath and exhale again, and take your body into a state of relaxation.

These calming techniques can be successful in reducing some of the emotional upset you have been experiencing after discovering your spouse's infidelity.

Changing Your Self-Talk

As you have already seen, the negative things you say to yourself are one of your greatest sources of emotional pain. "He maliciously deceived me." "I can't stand this." "How dare he ruin my life!" are examples of the hot thoughts that fuel your anger.

If your rage continues for a long time, chances are that the things you are telling yourself about what happened and its meaning are stoking your emotional furnace and keeping the coals glowing. Even when a genuinely negative event such as infidelity occurs, it is still the meaning that you attach to it that ultimately determines your emotional reaction.

To handle your anger constructively, you first have to identify the thoughts that generated it. Because anger is maintained by the statements you make to yourself, changing your "self-talk" will reduce it. By writing down your thoughts, you correct the distortions that contribute to your anger. Even though your thoughts may seem plausible and accurate to you, they may not stand up to closer examination.

To test the validity of your thoughts, ask yourself these questions:

- What evidence is there in support of my interpretation of his behavior?
- What is the evidence contrary to my interpretation?
- Does it logically follow from my spouse's actions that he has the motive I assign to him?
- What are some alternative explanations for his behavior?

Testing The Validity Of Your Thoughts

Thought: *Because my husband was unfaithful, he really doesn't care about me.*

EVIDENCE FOR THE THOUGHT	EVIDENCE AGAINST THE THOUGHT
He knew how hurt I would be if he cheated on me. He must have wanted to cause me pain, or he wouldn't have done it.	Even if I don't approve, executives cheat while on business trips. He could have been responding to peer pressure rather than wanting to purposely hurt me.
The fact that he was unfaithful shows he doesn't really care about me.	His behavior doesn't necessarily show he doesn't care. Most of the time he does show real concern and affection.

Conclusion: *After testing the validity of these thoughts, I conclude that although my husband was unfaithful, it doesn't mean he doesn't care about me.*

Another way to cope with your rage is to develop a stockpile of self-statements that you can say to yourself when you begin to feel angry with your unfaithful spouse. Following are some examples of how you might talk to yourself.

Calm Self-Talk

"Just stay calm. Getting all upset won't help." "I'll take a few deep breaths and relax. Feel comfortable and at ease." "I know how to reduce my anger. If I find myself getting upset, I'll just focus on my breathing."

Strategic Self-Talk

"If I start to get upset, I can check out what I'm saying to myself. So I might as well relax." "I can develop a plan to discuss what happened. What do I need to do first?" "As long as I keep my cool, I'm in control." "If I get too upset, I can always walk away." "It's okay to take time out rather than lose my temper." "I can always count to ten, then come back and talk about it."

Self-Reward Talk

"That wasn't as hard as I thought." "I'm doing better at this all the time." "Good, I'm hanging in there." "I actually got through our discussion without getting upset."

The best self-statements for coping with anger will probably be those you write yourself. Make them relevant and meaningful. Change them if they begin to lose their effectiveness. Keep your list handy at all times. Tape the most powerful ones to your refrigerator door, on your bathroom mirror, or in the inside flap of a purse or briefcase. Read them again and again until they become second nature.

Thinking Distortions That Fuel Anger

As you saw in the previous chapter, your thinking distortions have an important role to play in your emotional reactions. As with pain or depression, your interpretation of the event, the infidelity, may fuel your anger.

Labeling

One of the most common kinds of distortions that stoke anger is labeling. When you describe your spouse as "a son-of-a bitch," a "bastard," or a "damn louse," you are viewing him in a totally negative way. Dr. David Burns has called this particular error "monsterizing." If your spouse betrayed your trust, it is absolutely understandable to resent what he did. However, when you write your partner off in this way, you are ignoring his good points. In reality, everyone is a complex mixture of strengths and weaknesses. Labeling is likely to intensify the problems in your relationship.

Mind Reading

Another kind of thinking distortion that generates anger is mind reading. Although it may be natural to want to understand why your partner was unfaithful, your hunches about his "unconscious" motivation are likely to be wrong. Actually, it is very difficult to know what motivates another person. Some possible explanations you might offer for your spouse's infidelity are, "He doesn't love me"; "She's oversexed"; "I'm not a good lover, so she went looking for someone else." These guesses are likely to be invalid. In the heat of anger, you may not bother to check out your assumptions, and they may be incorrect.

Magnification

The third kind of thinking error that contributes to anger is magnification. For example, in the case of the "one-night-stand," the importance of it may be exaggerated. You might overreact and blow your anger out of proportion. As we have discussed, it is important to understand the type and the meaning of the affair.

Should Statements

The fourth kind of thinking error that fuels anger is inappropriate "should" and "shouldn't" statements. These occur when you find that your partner's actions were unacceptable to you and you tell yourself, "He should have known better," "This never should have happened," or "He should suffer the way I am." A fact that we will accept is that other people have free will and often behave in ways that aren't to our liking. Even though your spouse had an affair, he may not necessarily have set out knowingly and intentionally to create unhappiness for you.

Overcoming Your Internal Barriers

To confront your partner in a forthright manner requires courage. In order to take this important step, you must first overcome your internal barriers. Our clients have shared with us many of their fears. You may recognize some of your own in the following list.

1. Fear of Rejection. The fear that if I share my anger with my spouse, he might abandon me. If you suppress your feelings, you may end up sacrificing your self-respect. Your partner may perceive you as a doormat and fail to change his behavior. Ask yourself, "What do I want for the future, myself, and our relationship?" If you fail to handle your anger effectively, you are likely to feel victimized. You may lose what you want most from your spouse: honesty, sincere amends, and fidelity.

2. Fear of Conflict. The fear that if I let my spouse know how angry I am, he might retaliate. If you have learned that conflict is terrible and it is better to placate, you may tell yourself that speaking up is too risky. Rather than possibly evoking your spouse's ire, you may settle for "peace at any price." Unfortunately, the emotional price you pay may simply be too high.

3. Fear of Creating Worse Problems. The fear that my spouse may not be able to tolerate my anger. Some people do not speak up because they mistakenly believe they have to protect their spouse lest he drink, attempt suicide, or in some other way become shattered. Most people are not as fragile or vulnerable as you expect them to be. Furthermore, you are not responsible for your partner's reaction.

   If, however, your partner has demonstrated violent behavior in the past, your fear is justified. As we have discussed before, safety takes priority over all other concerns. Domestic violence is the issue that must be addressed first.

4. Fear of "What If." The fear that something awful, terrible, and catastrophic will happen if my spouse knows how angry I feel. If this is your internal barrier, we suggest you try to face your fears. Ask yourself, "What is the worst thing that could happen? Could I survive it?" Taking some risks will help you bring about changes in your relationship and increase your self-esteem. In the final analysis, self-confidence arises only through taking action and virtually never through avoidance. Not to risk means important issues in your marriage will not be addressed, and that is the biggest risk of all!

Expressing Your Anger Constructively

Constructive expression of anger is assertive, a response that lies between the two extremes of "stuffing it" and expressing unrestrained rage.

Assertive expressions of anger are moderate and directed at the right target, your offending spouse. They include statements of where you stand, what you want from the relationship, how you want your partner's behavior to change, and what is or is not acceptable to you.

Although we recognize that when you are angry, communicating assertively, rather than aggressively, is quite difficult, it is worth the effort in the long run. Resolving the crisis in your marriage will require a non-blaming attitude as well as a willingness to listen.

An important part of being assertive is making "I statements." For example, to say "I am angry and feel deceived" is a more productive expression of your feelings than a blaming "you" statement, such as, "You rat, you betrayed me!" Other expressions of anger our clients have found useful are:

"I am damn angry about what happened."

"I feel deceived."

"I resent hearing this from a neighbor."

Of course, even though you are making an "I" statement, there is nothing to prevent you from sounding angry!

A technique that you may find helpful for handling resentment has been proposed by psychiatrist and author Dr. Harold Bloomfield. He suggests that you write out a list of the resentments felt against everyone who has hurt you during the affair. You don't actually have to deliver your list of resentments. The very act of writing them out helps release your pent-up frustration.

In the final analysis, we believe that the most effective anger strategy depends on finding a middle ground between silent resentment and verbal or physical attack. Nondestructive expression of anger is not only important for your sense of well-being but it also enables you to make important changes in your relationship. The angry determination that "I'm not going to let this event ruin everything" can provide valuable energy to help you get on your feet, take hold of your life again, and make important decisions regarding your future.

Experiencing Jealousy

"These terrible thoughts keep going through my mind," said a deceived wife. "I keep picturing my husband holding her in his arms." "I wonder if her body is slimmer than mine—if her breasts are firmer." She paused. "I keep imagining them making love. Sometimes I'm so filled with jealousy that I can't stand it—then I start feeling sorry for myself all over again!"

When the person you love becomes involved with a third party, it is only natural to fear losing them and to want to protect your relationship. Jealousy has been defined as the thoughts and feelings that arise when a love relationship is threatened. It is the reaction you have when you suspect or have knowledge that your spouse is romantically involved with someone else. Jealousy may function as a warning that assumptions about your relationship need to be checked out.

You can also feel jealous of your spouse's work, consuming hobbies, or community involvement if it takes up time you'd rather he spent with you. One of our clients told us her husband pretended to work from two in the afternoon to ten in the evening. Eventually she discovered he was quitting at eight o'clock and playing pool with his cronies for two hours before coming home each evening. "I felt like the pool table was his mistress. I was jealous and I didn't know how to compete."

Much more troubling, of course, is the jealousy that arises from the discovery that your partner has been unfaithful. When infidelity occurs, you are angry because you have been deceived, and you may be fearful you will be abandoned. Most people view extramarital involvement as a serious threat to the relationship. It is understandable that you would react not only by feeling jealous but also by behaving in ways that seem out of character for you.

Many of our clients have described desperate attempts to control their spouse's behavior. Some of them have searched through their spouse's personal belongings looking for an unfamiliar name or phone number. Others have arranged for friends to "check up" on their unfaithful mate's activities. One woman appeared unexpectedly at her husband's office with a blonde wig and a clingy dress "just to let his secretary know he had a wife at home."

Other spouses have tried to check on their partner's thoughts or fantasies. "When we make love, you're really thinking about him, aren't you?" asks a jealous husband. Several of our clients have voiced concerns when their husbands watched attractive women on TV. Although these reactions stem from the fears that surface from infidelity, they can cause further problems in your marriage. Your spouse may feel controlled by your behavior.

Male/Female Differences

Studies of jealousy have revealed a number of male/female differences. Women, it appears, tend to feel jealous for different reasons than men. They attach greater significance to physical attractiveness in other women and feel more threatened by it. Men, by contrast, tend to be more concerned that the other man is a better lover. When men are jealous, they are more apt to focus on the sexual aspect of the affair, whereas women are more preoccupied with the emotional involvement of their spouses with others. When a woman has an affair, she is more likely to blame herself. A man tends to blame his wife, the other man, or "circumstances."

The Continuum

We view jealous feelings as falling along a continuum according to the degree of emotional intensity. At one end is apathy. The absence of intense emotion in a marriage can be as problematic as its presence. If a spouse discovers infidelity and is *not* upset, it may indicate there are serious problems in the relationship.

At the other end of the continuum lies pathological jealousy, characterized by overwhelming suspicion and possessiveness. Pathological jealousy can result in murder, as when blind jealousy led Shakespeare's Othello to strangle Desdemona. The attitude of the pathologically jealous person may be expressed as "You belong to me, and if you betray me, I'll get even with you. If I can't have you, no one else can."

Normal jealousy lies in the middle range of the continuum and is appropriate to the situation. A twinge of jealousy may warn you that your spouse is attracted to a third party and serve as a useful signal for the survival of your relationship. Normal jealousy is to be expected after your partner has been unfaithful, and it will continue for a while.

An example of how normal jealousy arises when the marital bond is threatened was presented in the case of our client Alene. Alene's husband, Cameron, was an emergency room physician in a local hospital. His fling with one of the nurses was discovered when Alene emptied a wastebasket and found a revealing note written by the other woman, Karen.

After the discovery, Cameron agreed not to see Karen and to work on the marriage. Alene, however, was not able to let go of her jealousy. Cameron noticed that Alene made a point of phoning him in the hospital cafeteria on a daily basis. When they were making love, she would wonder if Karen was still on his mind. In spite of Cameron's insistence that he was no longer involved with Karen, Alene continued to feel jealous and to distrust him long after the affair ended.

Alene's response to infidelity served as a healthy expression of caring and attachment. If she had not felt jealous, it might have reflected indifference and lack of commitment to the relationship. On the other hand,

Alene's jealousy needed to be managed well or it could further alienate Cameron and make resolving the marital crisis more difficult.

Managing Jealousy

A humorous piece entitled "Confessions of a Jealous Wife" by Judith Viorst describes some of the problems in managing jealousy. She notes that logic fails us when we are jealous, "and we do all the mean, nasty, scared, desperate and sometimes funny things that people do when they are feeling angry and hurt." The first reaction she identifies is "the stony-silence technique," a procedure that punishes the spouse while maintaining dignity.

The next technique, for those who "don't have the self-restraint to maintain stony silences," is the verbal assault, "which may range from rational discussion to sarcasm to outright denunciation, often accompanied by tears."

When rational discussion fails, violence may ensue, as in the case of her friend Connie, who decided that "if he ever tells me that he's having an affair, I'm going to grab the butcher knife and stab him right through the heart."

You may be a kind and gentle person and have thought of the butcher knife scenario yourself. That's what makes managing jealousy particularly difficult. It embodies a wide range of emotions including anger, anxiety, and pain even from people who are normally low-key. As we have explained, jealousy can be totally irrational, almost a form of paranoia, or it can be a valid, normal response to a perceived threat to your relationship.

"Perceived" is a key word here. Even when your relationship is not actually threatened, it is still possible to perceive it as under threat. Ask yourself, "What is it about the infidelity that you perceive to be the most threatening? Some of our clients have told us that they are threatened by the belief that the person they love is attracted or emotionally involved with someone else. They fear that their spouses care more for the other person and may leave. It is understandable that the threat of loss would be very upsetting to you.

One couple we saw, Aaron and Sophia, made an agreement they believed would help Sophia cope with her jealousy that sometimes came upon her with a force that shocked her. Aaron agreed to volunteer information about how he spent his time and also to answer any questions Sophia had concerning his whereabouts. Aaron knew that jealousy and trust were related because as trust grows over time, jealousy diminishes.

Aaron also decided to surprise Sophia with a gift. It was a gold heart on a chain, and he told her it was part of his apology. "Why don't you wear it and when that cloud of jealousy darkens your day, just touch it and know you are always in my heart.

"It seems appropriate. I know it's a symbol, and maybe it's corny, but it's sincere," Aaron told us. He was a man who was clearly remorseful and not embarrassed to make such a gesture.

Sophia felt that Aaron's understanding of her need to know how he was spending his time helped her to manage her jealousy. "It was nice being thought of with a gift, but actually it was helpful to know that when Aaron was absent and I couldn't speak to him, the heart was a reminder that I was still special to him. This is what I lost in his affair—my specialness. This is what makes me so jealous.

Managing jealousy involves sharing your feelings with your spouse in a nondestructive manner. By communicating in this way, we hope that a clearer understanding of the "ground rules" for behavior in your relationship will result. Handling your rage and jealousy ultimately involves rebuilding trust in your relationship, a gradual process that will require mutual effort.

Part III

Dealing with the Marital Crisis

Chapter 6
Decisions

If I am not for myself,
Then who will be for me?
If I am only for myself,
what am I?
If not now, when?
— RABBI HILLEL

"What am I supposed to do?" Marian asked the group. "Do I divorce him or go on with business as usual? Continue to cook his meals, wash his clothes, go out as a couple with friends? I have a constant pain in my stomach, I can't even look at him. He wants to play tennis this weekend, and I am thinking I want a divorce."

"I didn't divorce Ted," Cheryl reminded Marian. "I stuck around for the good life. Why should I give it all up to live poor? I look the other way."

"I couldn't live with that," responded Victor. "When I found out about Stacy's affair, I had to get to the bottom of it. I wanted to know why, and I wanted the whole thing to end. I wouldn't put up with it." The views you have just read are from people who are trying to make a decision about how to resolve their marital crises. You may be having similar thoughts and wondering about your choices.

Before making a hasty decision based on feelings of revenge, abandonment, or embarrassment, we would like to help you consider some important questions. Is your spouse willing to stop the affair? Can you and your spouse change the reasons leading to the affair? What is the significance of the affair to him? How will your decision affect your quality of life? How does your stage of life affect your decision? Are your fears keeping you in your marriage? Can the love in your marriage be strengthened? What is the impact of your decision on your children? What about AIDS and other sexually transmitted diseases?

Is Your Spouse Willing to Stop the Affair?

The first question that needs to be answered is: Will your spouse stop the affair? Some partners refuse to give up their lovers and present the spouse with a take-it-or-leave-it ultimatum. Others say they need a little time to figure things out before giving up the affair; and still others agree to end the affair.

Our view is that your spouse must agree to stop the affair and make a commitment to work on whatever issues led to the infidelity. If he will not give up the affair, then there will be a third person in all of your considerations. This maintains the triangle, and with it many problems that interfere with the resolution process. Giving up the affair means severing all ties with the other person. It means giving up not just sex but all contacts, including phone calls, letter writing, and sending messages.

As long as there is a triangle, the lover remains, at best, a distraction, and at worst, an appealing option of someone waiting impatiently in the wings. Unless there is a strong commitment to working together, communication and problem solving will be severely compromised, and the probability of ending the affair greatly reduced.

Inability to give up the affair is usually caused by ambivalence about it and/or the marriage. One client, Oscar, told us that he thought he could tolerate his wife's spending time with her lover as long as they were working on the marriage. "But it didn't work. It somehow took her energy. He was always there as a possibility for her. She couldn't decide if she wanted the marriage or him. Finally I called it quits when I realized she was working on the marriage out of guilt. She really wanted him. Guilt just won't hold a marriage together."

Giving up the affair can be difficult for you and your partner. If your spouse had an emotional investment in the other person, he will be grieving that loss. You will undoubtedly be hurt watching your spouse endure this pain as he grieves the loss of his lover. Many a group member has reported the agony of watching a spouse work through the depression over this loss.

This is a very vulnerable time in the recovery process. It is not easy to watch your spouse in pain over the loss of his lover. You may be ready to throw in the towel at this point. But we advise sticking with it. Remember, your spouse made the decision in favor of his marriage.

The commitment your spouse makes must be not only to give up the affair but to work actively to understand the kind of affair it was, why it occurred, and what it means to him.

Can You and Your Spouse Work Through the Reasons?

Although you are probably aware that currently almost one out of every two marriages ends in divorce, you may not realize that the statistics are worse for the second marriage. Sixty percent of second marriages fail. We believe one of the reasons for this is that people repeat their mistakes. The same ineffective patterns of interaction appear in the new relationship.

Because we view an affair as a symptom of a problem rather than its cause, we encourage people to work through the marital or individual issues before calling it quits. If, however, you try and you still are not able to make the marriage succeed, at least you will understand more about yourself and your marriage. By virtue of this increased understanding, you will be in a better position to make a wise choice in the future. This is an important accomplishment. In the next chapter you will find exercises that will help you deal with these issues and guide you through improved means of communicating, understanding, and relating to each other.

In addition to the marital and individual issues, you need to consider the reasons why the affair happened. Can these circumstances be changed? Some affairs leave little or no possibility for resolution; the exit affair, the poor-risk partner, the homosexual affair, and the family affair fall into this category. Other extramarital involvement reflects personal and relationship problems that can be corrected by working cooperatively on them, as in the case of transitional anxiety, need for attention, boredom, lack of sexual desire, and unfulfilled expectations affairs. The personal gain and the unavailable spouse affair can also be satisfactorily resolved, depending on the individual issues involved.

What Is the Significance of the Affair to Your Spouse?

A willingness to give up the lover is tied, in part, to the significance of the affair to your spouse. As we have discussed, a spouse finds it easier to end a fling than any other kind of affair. The serial lover may give up the current affair, but will he break his pattern? He may agree to do so, but the probability is high that he will not stick to the agreement. A romantic love affair involves deep feelings, so that many other considerations figure heavily in determining its significance. The spouse in a long-term affair may have established a life style that he doesn't want to change.

Although serial affairs lack emotional investment, they are high in significance because they occur for a long period of time over the course of the marriage. Such affairs occur with sexual addiction and poor-risk partners who have histories of stormy relationships and self-centered behavior.

The wife of a serial lover is in a difficult situation. She often tries to reactivate his interests in her by making herself more attractive and acting more sensual. This, she soon discovers, is futile. She cannot offer him the one thing he seeks—the excitement of a new woman to conquer without the restrictions of commitment and intimacy. Often, dramatic events such as illness, public humiliation, the death of someone close, or loss of status, such as through reduced income, cause the serial lover to stop his unfaithfulness. Although the prognosis is poor, it is not impossible to end this pattern if he is willing to work on it.

One evening in a support group, we saw an example of an affair that had little likelihood of ending when our client Pat said, "I don't want to hurt Peter, but I can't give Bernie up. Life is exciting with him. It's like a fantasy that's come true. I feel alive and happy just being with him. I really love him." In this case, there is little likelihood of a reconciliation with Peter because Pat is involved in a romantic love affair that she is reluctant to end.

Lovers find it difficult to end a romantic love affair because of the high degree of emotional investment in it. It seems that the obsessive issue for the unfaithful spouse is, "You only go around once. What should I do?" The lovers want to be with each other and usually make a decision that they must be together. The other spouse or spouses involved are devastated, not only by the betrayal but because they see the depth of caring the lovers have for one another.

Some romantic love affairs go on to become long-term affairs. If your spouse has been involved in a long-term relationship, you are undoubtedly aware that the length of time involved indicates a strong commitment to the affair. If you have been aware of the affair and have decided to look the other way, you have, essentially, made a decision to continue with the status quo. It may be the arrangement has occurred by default because you have not agreed to a divorce.

Although long-term affairs are difficult to end, it is not impossible to do so. Sometimes the third person has had enough of the no-marriage arrangement and leaves the relationship. When the affair ends, the couple needs to work on understanding why it occurred and work toward resolving the relevant personal and family issues.

How Will Your Decision Affect Your Quality of Life?

A question basic to the "stay or go" decision is: Will the quality of your life be improved or diminished without him? In assessing the quality of life, people often make decisions based on their values or beliefs about marriage, the family, loyalty, or religion. Usually the long-term affair develops because values and beliefs keep the couple from divorcing. On the other hand, marriages have ended for the same reasons. The key factor in making this decision is to understand what is important for you and the quality of your life.

Our client Evelyn decided to tolerate her husband George's affair in spite of the hurt and betrayal she felt. George was head of surgery at the local Catholic hospital and active in community religious affairs. Evelyn reaped the benefits of his reputation. She and their six children lived a privileged, upper-middle-class life, with family Christmas vacations in Aspen and summers in Europe.

Evelyn felt she had learned to cope with loneliness both from George's affair and his professional life. She carefully considered divorce, but decided that because of her religious views and her enjoyment of being "wife of," she could tolerate the affair. She didn't want to "live poor," she told her support group. George, on the other hand, had felt a divorce would hurt his status as physician and community leader. Although the decision was agreed upon by both, the hurt continued. Children and friends were aware of, and embarrassed by, their arrangement.

Evelyn's support group thought she was permitting herself to be treated poorly, but Evelyn had a different perspective. When she asked herself, "What would I lose and what would I gain?" she concluded she would be better off staying in her marriage. For Evelyn this was the best decision. Every person's case is different, and each must make his own decision after considering all the advantages and disadvantages.

Infidelity is only one aspect of the quality of your life. When it occurs, you may tend to focus on the affair rather than the entire picture, which includes the quality of life in your marriage. This was clearly brought home to us when Louise described her husband Louie. "I am the perfect mate for him—a real doormat. He's arrogant. He makes the decisions and controls the money. I get an allowance and have to ask permission for the car keys. If I am bad, I don't get the car. Yet when I found out he had a girlfriend, I was crushed."

Louise had entered into a lifestyle with Louie in which she had to be in a one-down position. Unfortunately, Louie would not participate in marital counseling. Louise came alone, and as a result of her improved self-esteem, she could no longer tolerate the quality of her life with Louie. She chose to leave the marriage.

How Does Your Life Stage Affect Your Decision?

The stage at which you find yourself in the life cycle often affects your decision-making and so becomes another consideration. A person with young children may be more inclined to give up an affair than one with grown children. We have seen many older women who have looked the other way when extramarital involvement occurred rather than risk age bias in the job market or worry about living alone. The fear of coming to the end of life and having missed out on some part of it is often the setting for an affair.

The story of Cynthia and Bennett illustrates decision-making that was strongly influenced by life stage considerations. Cynthia received confirmation of Bennett's affair from a private investigator she hired to follow him. He was seeing another woman, Marge, who was thirty-seven years old, a single parent, and a sales representative at Bennett's firm. She wasn't "any great beauty," the investigator reported, but instead, kind of "dowdy and sloppy."

For the past five years, Cynthia and Bennett had been having an age-related sexual problem. Although they had been referred to a sex therapist, they both felt uncomfortable about going, and had decided that sex was no longer important at their age.

Cynthia felt that she was to blame, and that if she were younger or thinner there would not be a problem. Had they gone, they would have discovered that no one was to blame, that their problem was the result of faulty interactions and/or thinking. Older marriages often need sexual rejuvenation and adjustments to accommodate the physiological changes that occur as people grow older. Rekindling fires through exploring new and shared interests often add the spice needed to enhance a long-term marriage.

Bennett refused to give up the affair even though he said he loved Cynthia and his attraction to Marge was physical. Cynthia believed that if he loved her, he wouldn't be having sex with another woman—and conversely, that if he was having sex with another woman, he must not love *her*. She could not accept this arrangement.

Cynthia continued in therapy to learn new skills and to understand what had happened in her marriage. She would have preferred to work on her problems with Bennett, but this was not an option. As she looked at the marriage more objectively, she was able to shed the guilt she had assumed. Cynthia realized that she could not control what had happened to her, but she did have some measure of power over her reactions. Because Bennett's affair was a fling, we would have expected a more positive resolution for the marriage. However, other circumstances had to be considered. In this case, Bennett's life stage was a major factor in his leaving.

Are Your Fears Keeping You in the Marriage?

Fears also influence how decisions are made. We remember Betsy, a client, who voiced what we had heard many times when she said, "I am putting up with his affair rather than be alone. I know he sees her, but he comes home to me. The world is made up of couples, and I don't want to be on the outside looking in."

The thought of being alone frightens many people. Yet, we have seen quite a few cases of people who have been living alone as a result of the high divorce rate and have conquered their fears about it. Many say it is better than they expected and that there are even some advantages.

As Tony told his support group, "I am really better company for myself than she was for me. I have lots to do. In fact, I really was lonelier in my marriage than I am living by myself. I still want a woman in my life, but I want stability and someone I can trust."

There are other fears that influence people to make a decision to stay in their marriages. We have seen many women stay for financial security and men for the stability of family life. Often a sick or disabled person looks the other way so that he does not lose financial support and the help of his caregiver. We want to emphasize the importance of examining these fears to see whether they are valid.

Can the Love in Your Marriage Be Strengthened?

"I don't know what love is," Maxine told the group at one meeting. "After his affair, I have doubts about it all. I don't trust myself to know if I love him, or if he loves me, or if love even matters."

Many of the women and men we have counseled feel the confusion that Maxine describes. They want to know what love is, as well as its role in affairs and marriages. You, also, may be concerned about these issues.

When Elizabeth Barrett Browning wrote the words, "How do I love thee? Let me count the ways," she did not anticipate that psychologist

Robert J. Sternberg, nearly a century later, would attempt to do just that. Dr. Sternberg reports that love has three major components: passion, intimacy, and commitment.

Passion is an intense physical feeling, sometimes described as chemistry, magic, or intoxication. Dr. Sternberg says that passion without the other two components of intimacy and commitment is not really love but infatuation. Passion peaks early in relationships and then drops to a lower level as the excitement fades and the lover falls off his fragile pedestal.

In growing up, most of us have been told that love is blind. To a certain extent this is true and can pose a danger to the marriage. When people are in love, they tend to idealize the object of their affections and see only the good qualities. We have seen that marriages based only on passion are in danger of ending or are vulnerable to affairs by one or both partners. When a relationship is based on passion only, the lovers may soon "fall out of love." As they get to know each other better, human failings become apparent. Faults like taking a long time to dress, which may initially have seemed cute, become annoying.

Successful marital partners, on the other hand, are able to give up their idealization of the lover, relinquish their unrealistic fantasies, and accept their mates "as is." Although passion decreases, the couple can work together and restore the excitement to their relationship.

The second component of love, intimacy, is the emotional aspect. It includes sharing personal feelings, thoughts, and fears with each other. Intimacy also involves closeness, communication, support, and a sense of trust and safety with the partner. Intimacy without passion and commitment is friendship.

The third component of love is commitment, and it is based on one's belief system, code of values, and the way in which one chooses to behave. Although commitment grows more slowly, it can reach the same heights as passion and intimacy.

Without the other two components, commitment alone, says Dr. Sternberg, "is empty love." Empty love is all that some couples seem to have left after closeness has been lost and passion dies. This form of marriage has been popularly called a "marriage of convenience." Often the marriage that coexists with the long-term affair is this type.

As you have seen, love depends on enhancing the passion of the relationship, investing energy in developing intimacy, and making a commitment. In a successful marriage, couples continually take stock and strengthen any components that have weakened over the years.

What About the Impact of Your Decision on Your Children?

Children are often a factor in keeping a spouse in a marriage. Our client Denise stayed in her marriage because of her sons. Denise had an affair with her husband's cousin. Although she was American-born, her husband was from another country with a very different culture. In another year they would be returning to his country to live. Denise told us how her husband discovered her holding hands in the garden with his cousin. The looks that passed among the three indicated that their secret was understood. Denise's husband became very cold to her after this, but he has never spoken of the affair.

She knew that if he acknowledged the affair, he would, according to his culture, have to divorce her. Denise, also, knew that her acknowledgment of the affair would isolate her forever from his family, and he would fight her for custody of her children. Male children are so valued in his culture that he would never allow her to raise them. Denise made the decision to give up her lover rather than her children. It was, for her, a romantic love affair. This man, Denise told us, was the love of her life.

Bart was another client who stayed because of his children. He came for counseling after he came home unexpectedly at midday to discover his wife, Penny, in bed with their neighbor, Jack. Bart had been a client three years earlier when Penny had had other affairs.

Penny had been unfaithful to Bart three times that he knew of and, he suspected, even more. She was never able to explain to Bart, or to herself, why they had happened. Penny felt that their sex life was good and that Bart was devoted, kind, and considerate. It may be, she concluded, that sex with someone else provided her with an extra feeling of warmth and security that felt good, although she acknowledged that sex with Bart gave her those same feelings.

Bart believed that the chances of Penny's behavior changing were slim and had nothing to do with him or with the way he treated her. He decided that by staying in his marriage until his son graduated from high school, he could be a stable influence in his son's life. In spite of her infidelity, Bart loved Penny and felt she was an exciting and beautiful woman.

What About AIDS and Other Sexually Transmitted Diseases?

The decision that Bart is making is much harder to make today than it was ten years ago because of AIDS. Given the lethality of the disease and the continuing rise in reported cases, those who look at infidelity as "fooling around" must join those of us who regard this as a deadly serious matter. Even more threatening than the infidelity is this new and silent demon.

Today, when married people take a lover, they could put themselves and an unsuspecting spouse at risk of death. The death toll is climbing from this virus, which damages the body's immune system so that it cannot fight bacteria and other microorganisms that invade the system.

Although partners of serial lovers have a higher risk factor for AIDS than others, all partners of unfaithful spouses may be at risk. Novels are filled with stories of innocent young women whose first sexual encounter led to pregnancy. Sadly, today there are stories of that first sexual encounter leading to AIDS, and then to death. No one in the infidelity triangle is free of risk, for today's demon is more diabolical. Lovers today who believe they are having sex with one partner may, in fact, be going to bed with more than one person, possibly two, three, thirty, or a hundred: as many as have passed the virus from person to person. Like our heroines from the novel, their story can turn into tragedy as the probability of contracting AIDS increases.

Honesty, denial, and looking the other way take on new meaning now that the incidence of AIDS is rising. The partner who is unaware of the affair does not have the choice of being, or not being, put at risk. Nor are other family members.

Clients Renee and Jim, childhood sweethearts, were married five years when Renee had an affair with her supervisor Larry. The affair had lasted four months when Larry accepted a transfer to another state.

A few months ago she received a call from the local public health service. Larry had AIDS and had named her as a partner. It was hard for her to believe that this was happening. She wondered how someone as professional and respected as Larry could have AIDS. Larry wasn't a homosexual or an intravenous drug user. He was an educated, middle-class man.

After much anguish, Renee was tested and found to be HIV-positive. The affair could no longer be kept secret. She had to tell Jim, but that difficult revelation was a minor horror compared to the situation the family now faces. Both her husband Jim and their little boy are also HIV-positive.

As the doctor told Renee and Jim, "The only way to know if someone is HIV-positive is by a blood test. A positive test means the body has formed antibodies after being exposed to the AIDS virus. It doesn't mean the person has the disease."

Although homosexuals, bisexual males, and intravenous drug users are at the highest risk for contacting AIDS, other people, like heterosexual women, can be at risk, her doctor told her. "Because we may not see symptoms for years after exposure, many think 'healthy-looking' means 'safe.' The only way to know if someone has been exposed is by the blood test, and there are some problems with that," her doctor continued.

"There is what we call a 'window effect.' This refers to the time it takes the body to develop detectable antibodies. So during this time a person can be infected and not yet show antibodies on the blood test."

The "window effect" was one of the issues that confronted another client, Grace, on the infidelity of her husband Merrill. Grace has been married to Merrill for five years, a second marriage for both. Merrill's work as a businessman required him to travel regularly.

Grace began to suspect him of being unfaithful. When she confronted him, he confessed and was contrite. He asked her forgiveness and promised to stop. He told her that there was no one person he was involved with; there were only one-night stands. It was the way, he told her, that he dealt with loneliness when traveling.

Merrill did stop his affairs for a short period of time, but Grace, who was very alert to the signals, realized that Merrill was continuing to "sleep around." She no longer trusted him and was concerned about AIDS. When she requested that he be tested for AIDS, he refused.

Grace was tested and found to be HIV-negative, but she still did not know whether Merrill was positive or negative. She was told that the HIV-negative results only accounted for the period up to three months before her test. She would have to wait another six weeks to three months without having sex with Merrill and then be tested again before being assured of safety. It might take that long for antibodies in a recently infected person to form.

She wondered, "Can I trust him to be faithful to me after he has been tested? If not, I can't really rely on what the last test tells me. He could be HIV-negative and then start screwing around again. I can't get him tested every week."

Grace is deciding whether she wants to live at risk and in fear. She has the option to stay married to Merrill, accept his infidelity, and practice "safe sex" by using condoms, knowing there is a 10-percent failure rate with them.

The possibility of contracting HIV through heterosexual contact has been steadily increasing in the U.S., especially among minority women. One must carefully consider whether to take such a risk when the consequences could be fatal.

Women in our group often talk about how demeaned they felt at having to be tested for sexually transmitted diseases, especially AIDS. "This is what my life has come to," one woman said. Another added, "I used to think of myself as a typical American woman with a husband, a house, 2.5 kids, a part-time job, and a shelf full of gourmet cook books. No one would suspect I am sweating out the results of an HIV test. I no longer feel typical. I feel dirty and discarded." Many of the women in the group could relate to what she was saying and were sympathetic to her feelings, but they all validated the need for testing for this fatal disease.

Other sexually transmitted diseases (STDs) such as genital warts, herpes, or chlamydia can also be by-products of infidelity. Many of these diseases can be painful and require uncomfortable and prolonged treatment. Some pose a risk of infection to the unborn child when the mother has the disease. Some STDs are not curable but can be managed.

Clearly the possibility of contracting a STD needs to be considered in your decision making.

How Do You Put These Factors Together?

The discussion in this chapter has been about some of the major questions you need to consider in making a decision about your marriage. There are others that we did not discuss because they are too individualized for such a general review. However, we would like to help you by presenting a method by which you can evaluate your options.

Let's look at the example of our client, Dee, who couldn't decide what to do about her marriage to Stan. Stan had a series of three affairs in five years. He promised to end the current affair and not to have any others. He refused to join Dee in marriage counseling because he said there was no problem. Some of the salient facts for Dee were that she loved Stan, they had three small children and a large mortgage, and their sex life was great. In addition, Dee was going to law school at night and struggling to maintain family life pretty much on her own.

We asked Dee to make a list of pros and cons about her marriage. This was her list:

PROS-for preserving the marriage	CONS-against preserving the marriage
I love him.	He's had three affairs.
He is a devoted father.	He promises to stop but
I won't have to drop out of law	doesn't.
school.	The quality of life is getting
Divorce would be a financial	worse.
disaster.	He won't go for counseling.
	He may be a poor-risk partner.
	I may be at risk for AIDS.

After discussing her list and "sleeping on it" a bit, Dee saw the case for divorce was stronger than the case for the marriage. She then had to look at the adverse consequences of leaving or staying in her marriage. Her next task was to decide whether she could resolve these consequences or mitigate their impact on her life. She concluded that she could not live with the risk of getting AIDS but that neither was she willing to give up her education or be in a tight financial spot. Her decision was to prepare herself for leaving the marriage by finishing her education and to practice safe sex with Stan.

Now let's take Myron's case. Sandy, Myron's wife, had an affair with their accountant, Lester. Myron had an excellent understanding of the circumstances that led to the affair. Myron knew that he had been too preoccupied with his lifelong dream of starting his own business. He spent long days, evenings, and weekends on the new business while Sandy was alone.

Sandy, he reasoned, was dealing with some major losses and midlife issues. The last child was off to college, and as a traditional homemaker, she felt at a loss for direction in her life. She had planned to open a catering business with her sister after their youngest child left home. Sadly, her sister had died the year before after a long and debilitating battle with cancer. Myron realized that Sandy was depressed.

"I was furious about the affair until I realized she was depressed. But it didn't take me long to figure out that I wanted to stay in the marriage. I had a previous short marriage when I was just a kid. Until this affair, I felt good about our marriage. I realized that I was so busy with my concerns about this new business that I just blocked her out. This was an especially difficult time for her, and I wasn't there. I believe this was just a fling. I am grateful she is willing to work things out with me."

Although Myron came to our support group without Sandy, they are working together on their marriage. In working with Myron in the support group, his thoughts about staying or going were the following:

PROS-for preserving the marriage	CONS-against preserving the marriage
I love her. She loves me. I understand the circumstances related to the affair. It was a fling. Sandy wanted to get my attention. Our marriage has been a good one.	She wasn't honest with me. It will take time to forget the pain from the affair.

If your spouse has agreed to stop the affair, you have the opportunity to heal the marital wounds and to work together to repair your relationship. If your spouse will not stop the affair, then you are not powerless. You still have options. If you desire, you can stay in the marriage and tolerate his infidelities, or you can choose to leave. It is also possible to postpone your leaving until you are emotionally and financially able to take that step. Whatever your decision, you can make a satisfying life for yourself.

Chapter 7
Repairing the Relationship

"Whom God hath joined together, let no man put
asunder."
— ANGLICAN MARRIAGE SERVICE

"I am not giving up on my marriage," said Diane, a member of our support group. "We have a history together. We have children, a home. We have too much invested in each other." Brian responded, "I know despite the misery that my affair has caused, I want to patch things up." Clark added, "I have to try. I couldn't live with myself if I didn't try everything I could." Genina said, "What scares me the most is that I know a number of people who are getting their second divorce. I think I'd better figure out what is going on with us."

Although we hear the pain in what they are saying, these people are beginning a healing process. We have seen many couples who have not only "patched things up," as Clark put it, but have turned their marital crisis into an opportunity to grow closer. Genina's concerns are not without foundation. The chance of a second marriage ending in divorce is greater than with a first. It seems that divorce may be only a temporary solution to individual or relationship problems.

We have seen couples who enter a second marriage with the best intentions but repeat the same patterns in the new relationship as in the old. We believe that you are better off postponing your decision to stay or to go until after you and your partner have done everything possible to improve or at least to understand your relationship. We suggest that you think of your marriage as a plant that has been overgrown by weeds. After pulling out all the weeds and nurturing it, the plant may flourish again.

If, on the other hand, you discover that you and your partner have significantly different expectations for your relationship, you may eventually decide to end the marriage. But first we suggest you hang in there and give it your "best shot."

Clearing the Emotional Air

In the preceding chapters we have shared some of our ideas for dealing constructively with your emotional reactions. It is only natural for you to let your spouse know how his dishonesty and unfaithfulness have upset you. But because your feelings are so intense, you may find them difficult to control. If your goal is to convince your spouse to end the affair and to work on your marriage, toning down your outbursts is essential.

As Lisa said, "I just wanted to yell and scream. I wanted him to know how much he hurt me. How could he! I just couldn't put it behind me and get on with my life. I needed something more."

What Lisa needed to hear was a statement of sincere remorse. Your spouse must acknowledge that he has cheated, agree to give up the affair, apologize, and express sincere remorse for the pain his behavior has caused. This is a vital step in the healing process. This apology must be forthcoming many times. People apologize once or twice for being late or forgetting a birthday, but more is needed when the marriage vows are broken. After your spouse admits his role, it is not enough to put it behind you and "get on with your life." We hope that this phase will come later, but to reach that point, it will take time and a commitment to work on the marriage. No other marital problems can be addressed, nor can the rebuilding of trust proceed, until you are assured that the affair has stopped and your partner is willing to make amends.

Apologizing

Although saying "I am sorry," is an integral part of resolving the affair, there is much more to it than this. When you apologize, you must be sincere, take responsibility for your behavior, show contrition and remorse, be empathic to the suffering that your spouse has endured, and include a promise never to do it again. This is only the first step in the process of apologizing.

Our experience with apologies is that, even with all of these requirements satisfied, the apology is not quickly accepted.

Jerome, a client, said in a group session, "I've told her a thousand times 'I'm sorry'. And I *am* sorry. I don't know what more I can do. I wish I could turn back the clock. I wish I could undo it, but I can't."

"Keep saying it," we told him. "She needs to hear it over and over again. And don't give up, because it will take a while before it is accepted."

If you are finding it difficult to accept your spouse's apology, you must remember that the affair has changed all your assumptions about yourself, your spouse, and your life together. You need to go through the process of recovery and understand the reasons why this happened, before you will be ready to accept your partner's apology.

Jerome's wife replied, "I hear his apologies. And I know he is sincere, but I have really been hurt and am just not ready to accept his apology."

Taking responsibility for having an affair is an essential part of apologizing. Those who blame their spouse for the affair further victimize the victim. Blaming by either person is counter-productive to resolution.

Additionally, the infidel must show empathy for the effects the affair had on his spouse. He must express appreciation for her pain, her disappointment, her fears, and her suffering. Telling her she is over-reacting, which we have heard said many times so as to reduce the importance of the affair, will infuriate her. This denies what she has experienced, and thus is the opposite of empathy.

Another woman told the group that she believes her husband would never apologize if he hadn't been caught. He says, "That's true. But now I am truly sorry because I see the havoc my behavior caused. "I am sorry," he told his wife. "I was wrong. It was a mistake."

Linguistic professor Debra Tannen, who writes about the differences in the ways that men and women communicate, states that saying "I'm sorry" is not enough. She points out that a statement that "I'm sorry I offended you" does not indicate sufficient contrition. Although it appears to be an apology, it stops short of admitting fault.

Professor Tannen believes that an apology is important because it affirms a sense of justice. In her view, it is particularly difficult for men to apologize because doing so "entails admitting fault and that shows weakness." Men more than women tend to be attuned to whether something weakens their position.

When President Clinton spoke to the nation on television for four minutes after his grand jury appearance, he apologized and took responsibility for his actions. The reaction to his speech was extremely negative because it seemed insincere and lacking in contrition.

The apologist needs to express his feelings as well. "I feel guilty. I feel shame. I am humiliated. I am sad. This is the worst thing I've ever done. I regret this." These are expressions of contrition and remorse, if spoken sincerely, and are components of an appropriate apology that also includes taking responsibility.

Reparations

In our practice, when one member of the family has deeply hurt another, we discuss paying reparations. This is the second step in the apology process. Reparations is a means of atonement, but it doesn't mean paying money. We leave it up to the couple to decide what they want to do.

Paying reparations doesn't come immediately, but rather when the reasons have been understood and steps have been taken to strengthen the marriage. The reparations that couples select require thought and must mean something to them. In one case, a husband wrote and framed a Bill of Rights for his wife because he felt he had treated her as though she had no rights. Some men have gone on their knees to ask forgiveness, with a promise that it will never happen again. Many reparations have taken the form of gifts. It is more effective if the gift has meaning. It is not to be misconstrued as a "pay off."

One woman asked for a necklace made of Roman glass found in Israel where the two had met. One husband gave his wife an animal sculpture to commemorate the safari they were taking after they felt they had closure on his affair. One woman bought her husband a puppy. When their dog died during the aftermath of her affair, it seemed to them like the death of their relationship as well. Now this new little puppy means a new start for them.

Forgiveness is the third and final step in the apology process. Although you may forgive your spouse, it doesn't mean that you condone the behavior or will ever forget the hurt. Memories of it will bring back the pain. Some people cannot forgive, even though their marriage continues and their problems have been worked out. Some clients tell us that they are disturbed by the fact that their religion requires them to forgive, and they have not been able to do that. We suggest that forgiveness may come, in time, but the most important thing is to resolve the issues and to reach an understanding of why the infidelity occurred and find ways to resolve the issues it brings up.

Who Is to Blame?

"I joined a health spa and worked out like crazy because I thought that was what he wanted," Maureen explained. "I dieted. I wore sexy lingerie. I became more active in bed. I tried to mold myself into a *Playboy* centerfold. I did everything I could think of to keep him interested."

Many of our clients have experienced a compelling need to figure out who or what is to blame for the infidelity. This is understandable. Peggy Vaughn, the author who discovered that her husband had been having a series of affairs, writes that when people look for reasons why their partners were unfaithful, inevitably they start with themselves. Anyone can find some real or imagined inadequacy to blame as the cause of their partner's affair. You may be looking for some personal shortcoming that might have caused your spouse to be unfaithful; for example, you may question whether you are sexy enough or attentive enough. Perhaps you wonder whether you are smart enough or sufficiently interesting to compete with the other person.

If you are able to avoid blaming yourself, you will likely blame your spouse. We have seen many of our clients place the entire blame on their partners. As Thelma told the group, "It's all his fault. I saw him flirt with her at parties. He chased her. He seduced her. If he hadn't been so immature and needed to prove himself, everything would be fine now." You may find yourself pointing out every possible weakness your partner has. The list may be endless. This is not an unusual reaction.

Finally, of course, there is always the third party to blame. But in assigning blame, there is seldom a direct cause-and-effect relationship. It is much more likely that the infidelity is a result of a combination of factors.

We strongly believe that you will be helped more through understanding than blaming. Blaming is similar to being on a treadmill: it gets you nowhere and you are exhausted from it. Recognizing that all affairs are not the same is a good starting point for understanding. Infidelity occurs for a variety of reasons. The problem may be either in the relationship or in the individual. Sometimes life stresses, opportunity, or the differing needs and attitudes of men and women have important parts to play.

Gender Differences

Consider the following scenario: Seth and Joan have been married for twelve years. It is evening, and they are getting ready for bed. Seth comes out of the shower and sees Joan under the blankets. He sits next to her, leans down, and whispers in her ear, "Hey, honey, you in the mood?"

Joan turns away from him and replies, "In the mood? Are you nuts? You ate dinner, read the paper, and vegged out at the TV. You didn't say two words to me all evening. And you want to know if I'm in the mood?"

Seth responds, "You're just a cold fish."

Like most men, Seth desires sex as a physical experience, although he may be emotionally involved as well. Joan, on the other hand, rarely enjoys a sexual encounter without romance, affection, and intimacy. Seth and Joan are exhibiting attitudes typical of their genders.

Infidelity is not always the result of dissatisfaction with the relationship, particularly for men. Psychologists Shirley Glass and Thomas Wright, who have presented workshops for professional audiences on restructuring marriages after extramarital involvement, report that gender differences exist and have to be accounted for.

If a woman has an affair, it is likely to be a reflection of marital dissatisfaction. By contrast, many men report that they are satisfied with sex and happily married. They are unfaithful for a variety of individual reasons, whereas for women the involvement is more often emotional.

Ann Landers, in her popular column, asked her readers, "Would you be content to be held close and treated tenderly and forget the 'act'?" A tidal wave of mail arrived. When ninety thousand women take the time to respond, it's clear that Ann Landers had hit a nerve. American women took the opportunity to make a statement of something they felt strongly about. Seventy percent of the women who said "yes" valued tenderness above having sex. Particularly interesting was the finding that 40 percent of the women who said they would be content without sex were under forty years of age.

"What do women want?" is a question that men ponder repeatedly. Yet it is no great mystery. Ask any woman, as many researchers and therapists have, and they will tell you: women want closeness, intimacy, and a sharing of personal thoughts, feelings, and plans.

A client, aged forty-five, once said to us, "If you would have asked me what I wanted in a man when I was twenty, I would have said, 'a hunk, a great-looking guy!' Now, after fifteen years of marriage, I'll tell you—it's communication. I want someone who will listen to me and talk to me."

Sometimes infidelity becomes a way for a woman to find caring, however fleeting, or to overcome the loneliness in her marriage and at the same time keep it intact. Studies show that women get more emotional satisfaction out of an extramarital affair than men, although they feel more guilt. For women, the verbal expression of feelings and ideas is central to their feeling loved and desiring sex, and a relationship without it is experienced as a deprivation. Women often have affairs to feel loved. Some women, aware of the power that sex has, may use it to attract a man because they believe it will establish emotional intimacy.

Women are uncomfortable with the dishonesty of hiding their affairs. As one woman in our support group said, "It's strange, but I feel worse about sneaking around and lying than I do about the infidelity."

Other women are concerned about their husbands' reaction, for good reason. Most men see their wives' unfaithfulness as an insult to their manhood, and as a result they are far less tolerant of it than are women. One of our clients said, "He has been having affairs for five years. In my unhappiness, I decided to have one too. I felt so guilty that I told him. The next day he saw a divorce lawyer."

Some men have affairs because they assume that the right to be unfaithful is simply a male prerogative, but they often have a hidden agenda of avoiding intimacy. Men who are uncomfortable with intimacy feel stifled or trapped as the relationship with a woman becomes emotionally close. Extramarital involvement can become a way for a man either to dilute or avoid emotional closeness with his wife. Alternating between wife and mistress is a way of avoiding intimacy with both women.

For some men, it is not a fear of intimacy but inexperience with it that leads to infidelity. When such a man becomes open and shares feelings or thoughts with a woman, he is likely to see the relationship as one with possible sexual involvement. Sex is one of the few, if not the only, means that some men use to show emotion. Men are discouraged from sharing their feelings, so that often all or most of their emotions, particularly tender ones, become expressed sexually.

Many men compartmentalize their sexuality and are able to put their infidelity behind them fairly easily. But because women's extramarital involvements are motivated primarily by emotional needs, they may find it difficult to comprehend how their husbands can separate sex from emotion.

From Blaming to Understanding

In our work with couples, we have observed a tendency for each partner to assume, falsely, that the other one views the world and other people in the same way they do. Recognizing the importance of gender differences may make it easier for you to come to terms with your spouse's behavior and, eventually, begin to care again. Understanding his actions does not mean you condone them. It is, however, a first step in moving from a position of blaming to one of understanding and mutual problem solving.

In the beginning you will probably want to learn everything about the infidelity and how it took place. Wanting to know all about it is a common experience. After one of our clients learned of her husband's infidelity, she told us about the anxious nights spent searching through his credit card receipts, checkbooks, and office calendar looking for evidence that the affair was still continuing. Her pressing need to know whether it had ended actually became an obsession.

In our opinion, it does not help the recovery process for you to hear all the salacious details of the affair. In fact, we have seen many situations in which brutal honesty impairs the process. Focusing on the details can prevent you from standing back enough to look for the causes of infidelity. It is working on these causes that will resolve the issues, not inundating yourself with the details. Your spouse will likely become defensive or "clam up" over these inquiries. However, because we recognize "the need to know" as being very powerful, we recommend the following "fishbowl" technique.

To repair the relationship and rebuild trust, we suggest that you and your spouse talk openly and honestly about what happened. Psychologists Shirley Glass and Thomas Wright have developed an approach for timing your need to know the details of the infidelity. It can help you avoid a destructive inquisition, to which your spouse is likely to respond by feeling trapped. Rather than relating like a detective investigating a criminal, you and your partner can use this approach to communicate like two people who want to understand each other better.

You will want to know who the third party was and how long the relationship lasted. Of course, you will also want to know whether your spouse was in love with the other person. Learning the answers to these questions is important because it helps you determine how serious the extramarital involvement was.

Whenever you think of a question you feel is important, write it down and put it in a fishbowl. Then, when you are not so angry and your spouse feels he can talk freely, he can go to the bowl and take out questions until he finds one he is willing to answer. It will be more productive if the first questions answered are simple information-gathering ones. If the question is potentially too explosive, it should be returned to the bowl. It is very important, warn Drs. Glass and Wright, to leave the more difficult questions until more closeness and trust have been built. Sharing details about the infidelity in this way sets up a safe environment and makes the disclosure process less destructive.

Strengthening the Relationship

One evening Angie confided her deepest fear to the group when she said, "I feel it's hopeless. How can we ever get back to where Kenneth and I were, after all that's happened? Our marriage is very shaky."

After so much turmoil, you may be feeling burnt out and somewhat hopeless. Like Angie, you may have lost sight of the positive elements in your marriage. We told Angie to picture a home on stilts, like those in the South Pacific. It's shaky, like her marriage. The goal of this visualization is to help build supports to strengthen it.

One way to increase positive feelings between you and your spouse is by using a technique called "Caring Days" developed by psychologist Richard Stuart. It can help you change your expectations for the future of your relationship from pessimistic to optimistic.

Initiating change with this technique requires that both you and your spouse participate. Waiting for your spouse alone to change is ineffective, whereas working together to improve your relationship demonstrates good will and commitment. Your joint efforts will help direct the emotional energy where it belongs, and as a result you will both feel more invested in your marriage. The ultimate goal of this technique is to rekindle the positive feelings you and your spouse once felt for each other.

Another advantage of this approach is that when you change your behavior, your feelings will follow. Have you ever reluctantly gone to a party and pretended that you were glad to be there when you didn't really feel it? Before long you begin to feel better about being there. What actually happened is that you acted as if you really wanted to be there, and your emotions changed. The same thing can happen with relationships.

Once you begin to do some positive things for each other, you are likely to gradually re-experience affection. By acting the way you think you would like your relationship to be, you can actually bring it about! So you and your spouse must act as if you do, in fact, care for each other.

To use this approach, begin by answering the question: "Exactly what would you like your partner to do as a way of showing that he cares for you?" Make your requests specific, state them in a direct and positive way, and make them small enough to be accomplished at least once daily. For example, the request, "I would appreciate it if you would be home for dinner by 6:30 P.M." is specific, direct, and positive. By contrast, the request, "I want you to show more consideration for me," is vague and difficult to perform.

We recommend that each of you list as many things as you can think of that your spouse could do to please you. Requests should state clearly what you want, such as, "Please ask me how I spent my day," rather than what you don't want, as in, "Don't ignore me so much." Try performing as many of these activities as you comfortably can each week.

There are other ways of showing your spouse you care, like bringing a small surprise gift, making dinner reservations, or buying tickets for a special event. We also suggest that you plan an evening out at least once a week. Make it a special occasion by planning activities that you both enjoy. Act as though you are just getting to know each other. Flirting is fine. Try to put playfulness into your relationship.

This approach encourages each of you to become responsible for improving the relationship without waiting for the other. By investing in your partner in these ways, you can begin to balance the negative feelings resulting from the infidelity with more productive ways of relating.

Reminiscing

Because you have a history together and have made an investment in each other, reminiscing can help strengthen your relationship. This approach involves setting aside an hour a week for you and your spouse to share positive memories. Make it a relaxed time with no interruptions. Have a cup of tea or a glass of wine, find a comfortable spot, and talk to each other. If any problem topics come up, write them down and discuss them at another time.

You can use the following sentence completion exercise for the first few meetings. You will want to eliminate any that are inappropriate and substitute your own.

When I first saw you, I thought . . .

I remember our first date. We . . .

The funniest thing you ever did (or that ever happened was) . . .

I think I first knew you were the one for me when . . .

I loved you for . . .

When we decided to get married, I . . .

The things I remember about our wedding are . . .

I remember our honeymoon . . .

When we got married, my life changed by . . .

I felt very proud of you when . . .

I remember how happy I was when you . . .

I remember when we first knew we were going to have a child . . .

I remember raising our children . . .

This exercise is intended to be positive and bring you and your spouse closer. Writing the story of your courtship and reading it to your spouse is another technique intended to strengthen your relationship.

One of our clients, Bonnie, wrote how she first met and fell in love with her husband, Robert. Bonnie and Robert were in their mid-twenties when they met at the hotel restaurant where they worked.

"Well, it wasn't love at first sight," Bonnie wrote, "but after a month of dating, I really started to fall for you. You were the strong, silent type, I guess. Just like they say, 'tall, dark and handsome.' Even mysterious, I would add.

"You took me to dinner, sent me flowers, and wrote notes. I remember one of them started out with 'You perfume the air you breathe.' Maybe it was corny, but I was really overwhelmed.

"We became lovers. You were a very passionate man, and somehow it affected me. I guess I felt grown up. I learned how good it was to be sexy. Before you, Robert, I never really got into it.

"One night you brought me a beautifully wrapped box with the loveliest nightgown and robe in it. They were ivory, covered in lace and pearls, and you asked me to move in with you. To me, it was like an engagement gift. I never lived with anyone before. And I accepted. Just like that! I didn't give it a moment's thought.

"It was heaven. It was so romantic. You gave me an engagement ring soon after that. On bended knee! And you even asked me for my hand in marriage. I felt like the luckiest woman on earth."

Sharing positive memories of your courtship can help you recall the mutual love and trust you once felt for each other. These reminiscences can begin a rebonding process and restore hope for the future of your relationship.

Discussing Your Backgrounds

Still another technique designed to help you repair your relationship involves discussing your backgrounds. Sharing what it was like to grow up in your family may help you to better understand each other.

One of our clients, Maria, talked about how her mother had warned her, "never let a man kiss you dirty." She understood that the messages she received from her mother contributed to her negative view of sex and inhibited her responsiveness to her husband. Another client, Ernie, shared how his experiences growing up in a conservative religious family made it difficult to be honest with his feelings. Still another client, Jay, described how his father had also cheated on his mother, which eventually led to his parents' divorce.

Following is another sentence completion exercise that can make your sharing process easier. Remember to eliminate any that are inappropriate and replace them with your own.

I remember my mother . . .

I remember my father . . .

My parents expressed anger by . . .

My parents expressed affection by . . .

Communication in my family was . . .

In my family it was important to . . .

My parents treated each other . . .

My mother treated me . . .

My father treated me . . .

The best thing that happened to me as a child was . . .

The worst thing that happened to me as a child was . . .

My brothers, sisters, and I . . .

To be noticed in my family, I had to . . .

My parents expected me to . . .

My parents hoped as an adult I would . . .

In my family men could . . .

In my family men could never . . .

In my family women could . . .

In my family women could never . . .

My self-esteem as a child was . . .

We have seen many couples who have found these discussions extremely valuable, not only for the important insights they provide but because sharing their experiences bring them closer to one another.

Rebuilding Trust

"I invented so many stories to explain my whereabouts, it was amazing that I was able to keep them straight," Lewis told us about his affair. "My secretary covered for me dozens of times. When my wife called, she'd tell her I was out of the office for an appointment, in a meeting that couldn't be interrupted, or unexpectedly tied up. You'd think my wife would have figured it out long before she found out about the affair."

When there is infidelity, as we have already discussed, lies are part of the territory.

Time away from home has to be accounted for. Since affairs cost money, stories have to be made up about extra expenses. Telltale clues have to be explained. One of our clients found her husband's soiled underwear balled up in the trunk of his car. He lamely explained that he had changed his clothes to play tennis and "forgot" them.

Many of our clients have told us that they don't know what's more painful, imagining their spouse having sex with another person, or the deception and dishonesty. Once you are committed to working on your marriage, in most situations lying will be counterproductive to rebuilding trust and repairing your relationship.

"How can I trust him again?" is a question we often hear from our clients. Because of the deception, understandably, it will take a long time before you will be able to trust again. But the trust issue involves both of you. You want to have faith that your partner won't cheat again, and he wants to trust that you will not remind him of his betrayal for the rest of your lives.

Trust can be rebuilt over time. It will happen gradually through honesty and openness, with words as well as actions. For example, when one of our clients, Irwin, accidentally ran into his former lover in the library, he voluntarily told his wife about it. He reassured her that he spoke only long enough to inform her that his marriage was in great shape.

For the unfaithful spouse, rebuilding trust will require an understanding that your partner is likely to be suspicious and want to actively question you. By honestly replying to questions or even anticipating them, you will begin to restore trust. You may not like this need to be open and honest, but it is necessary.

Adrienne told us in a support group that she realized that she was using her husband's infidelity as a weapon. "When he came home a little late from work," she explained, "I said, 'Did you stop off and meet her at a bar? Is it always going to be like this?' When I saw him grow red with fury, I realized how I relate every situation back to the affair."

Let's look at your belief system about trust according to the model we discussed earlier.

A *Activating Event*	B *Belief*	C *Emotional Consequences*
He had an affair.	He is untrustworthy.	enraged depressed hopeless
He had an affair.	Something went wrong. We need to discuss it and be more honest with each other.	angry disappointed hopeful

We believe that by acknowledging the impact of deception on your relationship and working together to turn things around, you and your spouse can begin slowly to rebuild trust.

Changing Your Defeatist Beliefs

"What's the use of trying? He'll never change. If he cheated on me once, he'll do it again." We have heard these comments from many of our clients. You may have similar thoughts yourself. One problem in marriages that have been touched by infidelity is the mistaken belief that things can never get better. If you have this pessimistic outlook, it could become a self-fulfilling prophecy and interfere with repairing your relationship. We want to assure you that many marriages can actually improve as a result of the crisis, especially when both spouses are willing to try. In *Love Is Never Enough,** Dr. Aaron Beck identifies several common "defeatist beliefs" that can make repairing your relationship more difficult.

1. My partner is incapable of change. It is valuable to recognize that people change, throughout their lives. We have seen it happen fre-

---

* From *Love Is Never Enough,* by Dr. Aaron T. Beck. HarperCollins Publishers. Used by permission.

quently in our work with couples. As you start to make constructive changes in your attitudes and behavior, you will find that you
can deal more effectively with your spouse. Once you and your
spouse develop new ways of relating, you are likely to continue
using them.

2. Nothing can improve our relationship. Dr. Beck suggests that this
belief can be tested. One way to do this is to identify specific problems in your relationship, then choose the one problem that seems
easiest to solve, and make whatever changes are required. It may
be as simple as agreeing to speak on the phone once a day. Even
a small change like this can provide hope that things can improve
between you.

3. Things will only get worse. After suffering so much pain and
anger from the betrayal, you may feel numb. We have seen spouses who are reluctant to risk closeness for fear of being hurt again.
To counter this belief, it is useful to look at the positives in the
relationship. For example, your spouse has stopped the affair and
agreed to work on the marriage. He is willing to discuss problems.
"Things will only get worse" is an example of fortune telling, the
thinking distortion discussed previously.

4. I've suffered enough. Working to improve the marriage can relieve
your suffering. By making a cooperative effort, you and your
spouse are likely to shift the balance in your relationship toward
happiness.

5. Too much damage has been done. The pessimistic view, that your
relationship cannot be repaired, needs to be addressed more realistically. You cannot be certain that your marriage is doomed until
you have worked to improve it. Some of the techniques we have
presented in this chapter might just make a difference. Try them.

6. My marriage is dead. By focusing your attention on the positive
aspects of your relationship through the exercises we have discussed, you may find that it is possible to revive your marriage.

Communicating Honestly

What does the infidelity mean to your relationship? What circumstances
were occurring in your lives, and what part did they play? How was your
spouse influenced by messages from childhood?

Although the answers to these questions may cause you further pain,
the alternative, not knowing, is worse. The process of resolving problems

in the marriage has to include honest communication. As your spouse shares information that will help you understand more about how the infidelity happened, the probability that it will recur decreases. You must listen, and both of you must be willing to accept your share of the responsibility for improving aspects of the marriage.

We would like to suggest that you set aside a specific time for these discussions. For example, you might talk to each other for an hour after dinner or every Sunday afternoon on a regular basis. The family atmosphere will become less tense, since you don't have to wait and wonder whether some accusation or incrimination will come unexpectedly and turn dinner into a battleground.

During the post-affair marriage, when you are feeling that issues surrounding the infidelity have been resolved, we suggest that you continue to use this time to be together and to share with each other. It will remain a forum for you and your spouse to bring up issues and differences, leaving the rest of the week conflict-free.

Communication means talking to each other about the likes and dislikes of your life together. It means taking the risk of putting marital issues that need to be discussed "on the table," openly and honestly.

Addressing Sexual Problems

Despite the fact that infidelity occurs for many reasons other than sexual ones, such problems in the marriage need to be addressed. For example, one woman complained to us that the only time her husband held her or expressed affection was when they were in bed. This caused her to lose interest and withdraw from him. Another woman complained that her husband was continually critical of her, which made her feel resentful and distant. An unfaithful husband told us that his wife was so involved with the children and her other activities that she had no time left for sex.

Some of our clients have shared with us that they no longer feel aroused by their spouses. One woman complained that her husband was a smoker who "reeked" of tobacco, which she experienced as a "turn off." A husband said that his wife viewed lovemaking as a duty, while his lover was "wild and passionate" and went out of her way to please him. Another told us that his wife was repulsed by oral sex, so he sought it outside the marriage. One woman explained that she sought a lover because her husband desired sexual contact much less than she.

Sometimes sexual problems are a result of unresolved problems in the relationship. Issues such as power struggles, fears relating to intimacy, unresolved anger, or poor communication may lead to sexual problems. In other cases, sexual dysfunction, such as disorders of desire, are individual matters that exist independently of the relationship.

An affair is a relationship that is idealistic and sheltered from the pressures of daily living. It is romantic because it is conducted away from the daily household responsibilities of sharing chores, raising children, and paying bills. It offers a sense of excitement and freedom that may be missing in mature marriages. This is one of the appeals of extramarital involvement.

You and your spouse can rekindle passion in your relationship by changing routines and sharing good times together. Some clients have told us they have rented a cabin in the woods or a room at the beach for the weekend for just the two of them, free of responsibilities and distractions. Others have planned romantic dinners in a restaurant overlooking the city lights. You, too, can think of ways to include time for romance and fun in your marriage. It's worth the investment. A point to keep in mind is that compared to a passing infatuation, your marriage offers mature love and shared experiences.

Forgiving

Although you may have painful memories for many years, the final stage of repairing the relationship is the willingness to let go of your resentment and forgive your spouse. Forgiving your partner's infidelity is different from condoning it. As your wounds begin to heal and trust is gradually rebuilt, you will be able to let go of the need for retaliation or revenge. Because the pain that infidelity causes is so intense, we recognize that forgiveness is not an easy process. It will, however, contribute to moving forward and creating new possibilities for the future of your marriage.

Recently, therapists have been finding that people can create meaningful ways to end a period and begin another in their lives through rituals. Rituals are part of all of our lives. They can help people move through transitions, close unhappy episodes in their lives, and open doors to new experiences.

Some of the rituals that quickly come to mind are engagement showers, retirement parties, and graduation exercises. Many rituals have a religious component. They underscore the importance in our spiritual as well as our psychological life. Some of these rituals are weddings, funerals, bar mitzvahs, and confirmations. Yet for many transitions and painful experiences, there are no rituals to help soothe our souls and bring peace of mind.

Divorce, miscarriage, and infidelity are a few such experiences for which there are no rituals.

We have known couples and individuals who have created rituals for themselves. An effective one came from a couple who wrote out their resentments, tore their list up, threw the little pieces into the river, and watched them drift away. Timing is important in rituals. You must be ready to let go of the anger for this one. We heard of one couple who buried their list in a nearby park but agreed that when they decided to blast each other, they would have to go to the park and dig up the list.

Dr. Evan Imber-Black, family therapist, described her work with a couple who had been unable to heal the pain from the wife's affair. She suggested they separately find an object or symbol that reminded each of them of "the unhappy time that had arisen between them." They were instructed to discuss the symbols and then put them in a large bowl of water and place it in the freezer. The next time they argued, they were told to stop the fight, remove the bowl from the freezer, and wait for the items to thaw before fighting about the affair. While they were waiting they were asked to discuss the positive aspects of their relationship. It was an especially helpful ritual because it provided an opportunity for their resentments to thaw as well. After the items thawed out, they could continue to argue if they wished.

The husband of one couple we worked with wrote her a long love letter. Whenever she started to obsess about the affair, she got out her letter and read it. This ritual was effective because he was remorseful, ended his affair, and made a commitment to his marriage. You can work together to create your own rituals. They can help you to let go of resentment and repair your relationship.

Some couples have decided to get new wedding bands or repeat their wedding vows. One of our clients who wanted to demonstrate his renewed commitment to the marriage juggled his busy schedule so he could arrange to take his wife on a "second honeymoon" to Hawaii.

• • •

Things will never be quite the same between you. Your relationship is forever changed. Despite this, we know it is possible to meet the challenge of infidelity and survive it.

Chapter 8

The Post-Affair Marriage

"Having an extramarital affair
Is like eating dessert
When you're on a diet:
The pleasure is short
The guilt is long
And the habit can
Ruin your life."

— *LOVE SECRETS FOR A LASTING RELATIONSHIP*, HAROLD BLOOMFIELD WITH
NATASHA JOSEFOWITZ

Making your marriage affair-proof for the future requires a combination of two basic ingredients. First, you and your spouse must both remain committed to preserving your marriage despite the suffering infidelity has caused. Second, you are both willing to examine your relationship and do what you can to improve it. When both elements are present, infidelity becomes a catalyst for change that can revitalize your relationship.

Recommitment

"Despite what happened, the thought of divorce never entered my mind," Howard told the group. "I was furious when I discovered the affair, but my commitment to my wife still means something."

Phyllis, married for twenty years, added, "I'll tell you why I don't consider divorce. I know there are some good parts to our marriage. I'm just too damned stubborn to give them up."

In the decision-making phase, commitment is the foundation, the bedrock, of a successful marriage. It is a promise to continue investing in the relationship despite pain and disappointment. Recommitment is an ongoing process. It involves the determination to stick it out and work through problems rather than give up. Each time you and your spouse grit your teeth and forge ahead in spite of obstacles, you are deciding to recommit.

Expectations

"I'm willing to forgive him and work on our marriage, but I'm scared," Faith told the group. "After what has happened, I wonder if we still want the same things."

In our culture, we have very high expectations of marriage. Like most newlyweds, you may have expected that the love between you and your spouse would exist forever with very little effort to help it along on either of your parts. You may have unrealistically expected that when your prince or princess arrived, you would live "happily ever after." Perhaps your expectations were more practical; somebody to provide an income, raise children, arrange social activities, and enjoy sex with you. As marriages mature, expectations often change.

"Twenty-five years ago when William and I were married, I quit my job to stay home and raise our kids. I was a traditional mom, and he was the breadwinner. Things have changed. I got interested in politics and the women's movement. To my surprise, I've become a political activist. The kids are gone, and I don't want to stay home," Mildred told us.

William shook his head sadly. "What does she need me for? She can take on the whole system. I think that was the problem. So I found a traditional woman, and for a while I felt good about myself."

William and Mildred, like most couples, did not take change into account. Individuals, families, and social conditions do change, and as a result, marriages must bend and flex a little to accommodate the changes. Ongoing discussions, such as the one William and Mildred are engaged in, can be part of the recommitment process.

What were your initial hopes and dreams for your future when you married? Knowing that change and growth are part of living together, we suggest that you and your spouse discuss what you each want to get from your marriage and how you will integrate the changes.

Many couples assume without ever actually checking it out that their partner shares their expectations and goals. The following list of common expectations of marriage was adapted from the work of psychiatrist Dr. Clifford Sager. It may help you discover some things you want from your spouse you have never discussed.

Beside each item, mark *YES* if it is still an important expectation for you, *NO* if it is not, or *?* if you are not certain how you feel or it is not relevant to you. We suggest you and your partner each complete the list privately and then share your answers. We want to caution you, however, that no one's marriage can live up to all the expectations on the list.

1. A partner who will be loyal, devoted, loving, and trustworthy.
2. A support against the rest of the world. Someone to stand by me in times of need.
3. Companionship and protection against loneliness.
4. Security, calmness, and order. A refuge from the stress of daily life.
5. A lifelong commitment.
6. Sexual exclusivity.
7. Lovemaking whenever I desire.
8. Creation of a family and the experience of reproducing and raising children.
9. A respectable position and status in society.
10. An economic partnership.
11. A partnership which builds and plans for the future together, which in itself gives meaning and purpose to life.

After you and your spouse have each completed the exercise, we suggest you review the list and discuss the following questions.

- How have your expectations changed through the years?
- How realistic are they?
- Which expectations are most important to you?
- How do your expectations differ from your spouse's?
- How can you resolve your differences?
- What expectations do you want to add to the list?

By clarifying your expectations for the post-affair marriage, you and your spouse can begin to move forward. This process can help you establish your future "ground rules" and rewrite your marital contract.

Resolving Differences

After completing the preceding exercise, you may have been surprised to find that you and your spouse had a number of conflicting expectations. In our work with couples, we have found that the way differences are resolved is more important than how compatible a couple is.

As Sam told us, "Religion has always been an issue for Becky and me. Becky is very observant, and I am not. It was hard, but we worked out a way to coexist around our differences. It involved my learning to respect her devotion and her not trying to change me."

Religious differences are often points of major dissension for couples, but Sam and Becky learned to live with incompatibility. Differences in politics and philosophies about raising children are examples of areas that often strain relationships.

No two people can agree on every issue. Although no one likes it, living together involves resolving differences. You may have been trained from childhood to avoid conflict. "Don't make a big thing out of nothing"; "If you can't say anything nice, don't say anything at all." Like others you may have heard these messages and learned them well. To quote Charlie Brown, of *Peanuts* fame, "No problem is too big you can't run away from it."

Unfortunately, running away from conflict can only hurt your relationship. First, you may deprive yourself and your partner of mutual knowledge, and he can't learn how you feel about an issue if you don't share it. Second, when you allow conflict to go underground, you never know when or where it will surface in indirectly expressed hostility. Finally, if an important problem is ignored, it can become increasingly difficult to handle.

The following uncompleted sentences are intended to help you discover the typical ways you respond to confrontations. We suggest that you and your spouse complete this exercise together and discuss your responses. This way you will have an opportunity to deepen your understanding of each other's reactions.

Confrontation means . . .

When someone avoids confrontation with me, I . . .

I sometimes avoid confronting someone when . . .

When I confront someone I care about, I . . .

When I confront a difficult person, I . . .

I feel most vulnerable during a confrontation when . . .

I feel most confident during a confrontation when . . .

The time I handled confrontation least effectively was . . .

The time I handled confrontation most effectively was . . .

When I confront you, I . . .

When I decide not to confront you, it is because . . .

It would be easier to confront you if . . .

When you confront me, I . . .

Some of the conflicts we have successfully resolved in our marriage include . . .

Some of the conflicts we have not yet resolved in our marriage include . . .

I believe I could deal better with our differences if I . . .

Airing differences can lead to mutual problem solving. Of course, the way in which you air them will contribute significantly to the outcome. Professors Jeanette and Robert Lauer surveyed 351 couples who said they were still happy together after fifteen or more years of marriage. These happily married couples agreed that intense expressions of anger, resentment, and dislike were damaging to a relationship. Only one couple in the survey said they typically yelled at each other. The rest emphasized the importance of restraint. They believed that a certain calmness is necessary in dealing constructively with conflict.

One participant in the survey offered wise advice. "Discuss your problems in a normal voice. If a voice is raised, stop. Return after a short period of time. Start again. After a period of time, both parties will be able to deal with their problems and not say things that they will be sorry about later."

If a conflict degenerates into an insult exchange or becomes a repetitive, stale argument, then it is obvious that no new solutions are being provided. Instead, try brainstorming to generate some alternatives that you can both live with.

Brainstorming is a useful tool to resolve differences. This is how it works. You and your spouse set aside time to freely suggest and write down every possible solution you can imagine to resolve your conflict. During the brainstorming session, the guiding rule is that neither one of you should criticize each other's suggestions. This absence of criticism encourages each of you to express imaginative and fresh ideas without fear of being judged. When you are finished, discard the impractical suggestions and consider implementing those that have some constructive possibilities.

Uncomfortable as conflict can be for some people, confronting and resolving problems is more effective in the long run than evading them. When couples are able to be mutually respectful, neither partner wins at the other's expense, and the real winner is the relationship.

Negotiating Compromises

Being willing to listen to each other and negotiate compromises is vital to all marriages, but especially to the post-affair marriage. You negotiate for what you want all the time. When you and your friend decide on a place to meet for lunch or your husband agrees to stop his affair so you will not leave the marriage, you are negotiating compromises. In negotiated compromises, neither partner sacrifices basic integrity and both get some of their "needs" met. Compromises may take several different forms.

The first form of compromise is one in which one person gets his "needs" taken care of immediately while the other person gets taken care of later. In other words, you and your spouse agree to take turns. The deal is "this time we'll do it your way, and next time, my way." For example, one weekend you might attend a concert your spouse recommends, and the next weekend you might arrange the hike in the woods that you prefer.

A second form of compromise involves each of you giving up something. For example, you might attend an outdoor concert and then take a short walk. If your spouse wants a sports car and you want a station wagon, you might agree to buy a sedan. In other words, you agree to meet each other someplace near the middle.

The third form of compromise involves trading two nonnegotiable items. Such an item is something you are unwilling to give up under any circumstances. In other words, there are some things that you feel so strongly about that you are unwilling to meet your spouse halfway on them. He also may have such items. By trading nonnegotiable items, you can avoid a stalemate and arrive at a mutually acceptable compromise.

Reestablishing trust is one of the most difficult tasks in the post-affair marriage. If the person with whom your spouse had an affair was a coworker, an example of a nonnegotiable item could be insisting that he give up his Friday after work "happy hour" outings. His nonnegotiable item in exchange could be for you to let him unwind for about twenty minutes when he comes home from work before requesting conversation.

In order to implement a compromise, a formal contract may be written up with rewards for successful participation and penalties for noncompliance. Some examples of rewards are material rewards (gifts, special meals), social rewards (attention, affection) and behavioral rewards (running errands, doing favors).

Sample Contract

I AGREE TO	YOU AGREE TO	COMPLIANCE REWARDS	NON-COMPLIANCE PENALTIES
Let you unwind quietly after work for twenty minutes.	Stop attending "happy hours" after work.	He will get total body massages twice a week.	He will do grocery shopping for a month.
		She will get breakfast in bed on Sundays.	She will mow the lawn for a month.

The preceding is a sample contract. You and your spouse should try to be specific in coming up with possibilities for rewards and punishments. In order to work out compromises, you don't necessarily have to draw up a written contract, but you do have to be willing to listen and communicate your requests clearly to your spouse and generate ways to meet each other's needs that are mutually respectful.

Improving Communication

In marriages that have been affected by infidelity, many couples have difficulty communicating with each other effectively. Good communication involves expressing your feelings openly and directly as well as encouraging your partner to express his feelings. We have identified a number of myths that block effective communication. Recognizing these myths may help you and your spouse improve your communication.

> Myth 1: Couples ought to know what the other thinks, feels, or wants. Your partner does not have a crystal ball. You need to let him know directly.

Myth 2: Couples ought to agree with each other after they have discussed an issue. Two human beings of the opposite sex with different life experiences are not likely to see eye to eye on every issue. Sometimes you may agree to disagree. A statement like, "I guess we see it differently" can be helpful on occasion.

Myth 3: Discussing your problems means you must now solve them. Some problems don't have a solution but require understanding. For example, your wife may just want you to understand how upset she feels. Your husband may want you to be willing to listen to his explanation of what happened.

Myth 4: Sharing feelings means your partner must act to do something. Your partner can acknowledge that he hears you but still exercise his right to say "no" to your request. He might propose a compromise or want to think about the issue further.

Myth 5: Rejection of my views means a rejection of me. This is an example of the thinking distortion called "personalization." If your spouse disagrees with your opinion, he is seeing things in his own way. He may disagree with your point of view on an issue. This doesn't mean he's rejecting you as a total person.

Myth 6: Doing what your partner wants doesn't count if you had to be told to do it. Effective communicators exist. Mind readers don't. The easiest way to get your needs met is to ask directly for what you want.

Myth 7: In true love partners can sense the other's needs. This is another example of expecting your partner to be a mind reader. It may also reflect an implicit "should statement," another cognitive distortion. Perhaps you believe that if your partner really cared about you he *should* intuitively know what you need. Few people are naturally that intuitive. When you state your needs directly, you eliminate the possibility of misunderstanding.

Myth 8: Love means never having to say you're sorry. This may be a pithy line of dialogue in a movie, but it isn't an example of effective communication. Apologizing when you've made a mistake indicates that you are taking responsibility for your actions. It also shows your partner that you care about his feelings. Apologizing is essential when a spouse has been unfaithful.

Revitalizing Your Sexual Relationship

By definition, infidelity involves extramarital sex. Part of recommitting to the marriage is revitalizing your sexual relationship.

Communicate Your Needs

In our groups we have heard comments like, "After nine years of marriage, he should know I love having my ears kissed. You'd think he'd catch on by now." "She says she wants me to be a 'good lover,' but I'm never sure what she wants. I wish she'd tell me what to do to please her."

Revitalizing your sexual relationship begins with openly communicating to your partner what would please you and what arouses you. Luanne complained, "I don't feel part of our lovemaking. I feel like an object, like a board with a hole in it. He doesn't hold me or cuddle." We encouraged her to let him know directly that she needs to feel "turned on." A husband who had a fling with his secretary told us his wife "just lies there" and is too embarrassed to tell him what she wants.

When you openly communicate your sexual preferences, you relieve your partner of the burden of mind reading. Communicating includes making requests, telling your partner what feels pleasurable, and describing your unique sensual and sexual desires. It appears that the key to a satisfying sexual relationship with your spouse depends on letting him know what "turns you on."

Some examples of this kind of heart-to-heart communication are:
"What I really want most of all is just to be held."
"I want to make love with the lights on."
"I want you to say nice things to me when we make love."
"I'd like you to wear a sexy teddy and take the initiative in sex."
"I get turned on when you . . ."
"It makes me feel uncomfortable when you . . ."

It is especially important in bed to communicate your feelings. Some people have told us that talking during lovemaking spoils the mood for them, while other find it enhances their experience. Still others prefer to communicate to their partners nonverbally through the use of body movements. Whichever way is more comfortable for you and your partner, communicating your sexual preferences is essential to achieving sexual compatibility.

Some people are not fully aware of their sexual preferences and are uncertain what to ask their spouse to do to please them. By softly touching, stroking, and fondling each other, you might spend many pleasurable hours in mutual sensory discovery. Many couples, in their fixation on the sexual act, forget about the rest of their bodies. In sessions of approximately twenty minutes for each of you, try pleasuring your partner without actually touching the genitals. You should allow yourself to enjoy receiving pleasure without rushing to return the favor. In this way you can learn to feel and respond to simple touching and stroking and to communicate to your spouse what sensory experiences are pleasurable.

Enhancing Sexual Enjoyment

A common problem in any long-term relationship is how to keep alive the physical and emotional attraction that originally brought you and your mate together. Lingering resentments about your spouse's infidelity as well as worries about jobs, finances, children, or other distractions of daily life can interfere with sexual enjoyment in marriage.

A long-term sexual relationship can easily become routine if it assumes a same time, same place, same activity quality. Many couples have complained to us that their sex life has become dull, with little variety and a narrow repertoire of sexual activities. Enhancing sexual enjoyment requires time, planning, and preparation. Keeping sex an adventure in the post-affair marriage presents you and your spouse with both a challenge and an opportunity for discovery.

Many people have fantasies of new sexual activities they would like to try but are embarrassed to share them with their spouse. Describing your X-rated fantasies to each other can add new dimensions and excitement to lovemaking. Fantasies might include "turn-ons" you've always wanted to try as well as those you might never want to actually experience, even if you had the opportunity. After sharing them, you and your spouse might decide to act out some of your sexual scenarios. We want to reassure you that there is no such thing as an objective standard for sexual preferences. What turns one couple on turns another off.

In her book *For Each Other*, psychologist and sex therapist Dr. Lonnie Barbach describes a complete program for improving your sex life. We will share a few of her suggestions for enhancing sexual enjoyment that you and your spouse may want to experiment with.

Creating a sensual scene can enhance your lovemaking. Satin sheets and pillowcases can help excite your sense of touch. Candlelight can create a relaxed and romantic setting. Making love on a blanket in front of a warm fire in your fireplace can be erotic. Try making love in different places in your house. Some people find the pleasant scent of soaps, powders, and colognes arousing. Many women feel that cleanliness plays an important part in feeling sexually turned-on. They like to be clean and prefer that their partner has showered also. Taking baths or showers together can become a sensual experience.

For some partners, negligees and sexy underwear are arousing. Romantic music can also help to set a mood for lovemaking. Giving a sensuous massage with scented oil, watching an erotic video together and discussing your reactions, or going away for weekends to different romantic places can help you and your spouse realize your full potential for sexual expression.

Relating Out of Bed

To feel in the mood for lovemaking, sometimes what you want from your spouse is nonsexual. Many women place the importance of romance, including hand-holding, hugging, and kissing, above techniques. In order to respond to a man sexually, women tell us they want to feel respected, valued, and above all, loved.

It is very easy to get caught up in the myriad details of everyday living. When this happens, your marriage can take on the aspects of running a business. Therefore, we suggest you and your spouse make a conscious effort to improve your relationship in six basic areas. You need to connect with each other emotionally, intellectually, and socially. You also need to make time for fun, humor, and spontaneity in order to put more joy in your marriage.

Relating Emotionally

In the previous chapter we discussed the importance women place on emotional intimacy. Emotional closeness involves such things as sharing, communication, and support. It means you are concerned about your spouse's welfare and want to meet his needs as well as your own. It also includes self-disclosure, sharing with your spouse the most private details of your life, and a willingness to face challenges to your relationship, such as infidelity.

Relating emotionally involves two-way communication. By listening and paraphrasing what your partner has said, you can let him know you've understood. Listening is an attempt to see the world through another person's eyes. Two-way communication also involves expressing your feelings, wants, and desires.

Many people fail to achieve true intimacy with their partners because they play roles and hide behind facades. They want so much to be loved that they conceal any feelings that may mar their image. Relating emotionally also includes trying to please your partner and demonstrating your affection.

Relating Intellectually

You relate intellectually when you share your thoughts and ideas with your partner. Try including discussions of politics, religion, or current events in your relationship. Learning new things together, sharing a book you've read or an article in the paper, and attending lectures, plays, or movies together can all enrich your marriage. Try spending a regular time together in which you share ideas. Earlier in this chapter we suggested that you and your spouse discuss your expectations for your life together. This is also a way to relate intellectually.

Keep informed about each other's areas of interest. One of our clients, Herman, told us how close he felt to his wife Emma when she expressed interest in his work as a computer engineer. Although he doubted that Emma had understood much of the technical parts of his discussion, the interest and enthusiasm she conveyed made him feel that she genuinely cared about how he spent his work life.

Moira and Sheldon connected intellectually by sharing their passion for dogs. They each knew the standards for the various breeds recognized by the American Kennel Club and enjoyed attending dog shows. This common interest provided the basis for an intellectual connection.

Relating Socially

You and your spouse must be able to share a social life. Having friends in common provides a support system for your relationship. Relating socially may involve joining a church, playing on a softball team, or volunteering for a community organization together to make new friends. One of the couples whose marriage was impacted by infidelity joined a church chorus together and made a new circle of friends. Another couple became active in a square dancing group and enjoyed many new friendships. Consider keeping social events on a calendar and planning ahead to get together with friends.

Some couples have told us they enjoy spending a lot of time together. Companionship and sharing activities is an important part of a healthy marriage. Of course, spending mutually enjoyable time together usually takes a combination of planning and imagination. One couple charged all their groceries, gas, and telephone expenses on an airline-sponsored credit card so they could earn free miles and plan an interesting trip each year. Another couple enjoyed visiting antique stores and decorating their house. Still another shared an interest in gardening and spend many weekend afternoons shopping for plants and working in their yard. Sharing social activities can foster a sense of togetherness.

Have Fun Together

Successful marriages involve having more fun with each other than with other people. You and your spouse can experience pleasure in your life together by recognizing that you are committed not only to the responsibilities of marriage but also to the fun and playfulness of being together. By putting more joy in your marriage, you can help to make it affair-proof for the future.

One additional finding in the Lauer's survey of successful marriages was that, in addition to a belief in marriage as a long-term commitment, laughing together was especially important. Perhaps you and your spouse can recall humorous incidents from your last vacation, a family celebration, or some other occasion. Share them. Norman Cousins claimed to have cured himself of a terminal illness with, among other things, the power of laughter. Victor Borge said, "laughter is the closest distance between two people." It can overcome inhibitions and tension in your relationship.

Include Spontaneity

The word *spontaneous* is derived from the Latin *Sua Sponte*, which means "coming from within." Spontaneity is the free emergence of that which comes from within you. Some examples of spontaneity that can flow freely in your relationship include sharing ideas, flashes of insight, or unplanned activities. Spontaneity means deciding to have a picnic on a sunny afternoon, visiting a friend on short notice, or calling up another couple and deciding to meet for pizza "at the last minute." Although there's nothing wrong with planning ahead, spontaneity can contribute to a successful marriage.

Other examples of spontaneity include giving each other surprise gifts, making arrangements for unexpected activities, or preparing a special meal that your spouse particularly enjoys. One wife wrote humorous notes and stuck them in her husband's lunch. A husband surprised his wife with flowers. Doing things that neither of you expects can help keep your marriage interesting and alive.

Loving Again

"When I was with Dan, my lover, I felt he accepted me for myself. He didn't judge me or criticize me. He liked me just the way I am," Winnie told the group. "I had the same experience," Nancy added. "I felt I could talk to Mort like a friend. There weren't any hoops that I had to jump through. I could just be myself. I felt loved."

Loving again involves seeing your spouse as he is and accepting his unique individuality without trying to change him. When we love and accept another person, we care for his welfare and enjoy being with him.

List Your Partner's Positive Qualities

When you and your spouse fell in love, you appreciated each other's positive qualities. One common problem we observed in marriages that have been touched by infidelity is a tendency to focus on what is missing from the relationship rather than on what you are getting from it. Making a list of your partner's positive qualities may help you get in touch with loving feelings.

One of our clients generated the following list of her husband's positive qualities:

1. good sense of humor
2. handsome
3. intelligent
4. hardworking
5. sexy
6. affectionate
7. cooperative
8. good conversationalist
9. generous
10. good father

Remember, if you want to improve your relationship, it's a good idea to start with positives. Focusing on them doesn't mean there aren't areas of your relationship that still may need work, but repeated reference to the list can help you gain a more balanced view of your partner.

Love Days

One way to begin the process of loving again is to try a strategy reported by Drs. Jacobson and Margolin called "love days." This technique has some similar features to the "caring days" approach previously described. It differs, however, in several important respects. Rather than giving small pleasures to each other consistently over a period of several days, the "love days" strategy stacks them up, and the effect tends to be more dramatic.

In this approach, you and your spouse are assigned separate love days. On that day, the person giving the love day attempts to be exceptionally pleasing, independent of the actions of the partner. Of course, the giver needs to be familiar with his spouse's preferences and prepared with an array of pleasing events in order to make the love day a success. A simple variation of this approach is to set aside briefer periods of time, "love hours" or "love evenings," with the same goal, providing pleasant experiences for your partner.

Although Arnie, a former client, wasn't aware of the "love days" strategy, he described just that when he told us how he designed a special day for his wife. "I hired a sitter," he told us "and then called Margot and told her to dress for a day out. I planned brunch, a day at the Smithsonian, and then a walk around the canal in Georgetown. It was one of those spectacular autumn days in Washington where just walking through the fallen leaves makes you glad to be alive. Then we finished the day with a drink at a wonderful French restaurant in Great Falls, Virginia. I felt really proud that I thought of this. It was a special day that has become part of our memories," he concluded.

Dr. Leo Buscaglia wrote several books about love. *Living, Loving and Learning,* a collection of his lectures, includes a description of the qualities of a loving relationship that we want to share with you as you and your spouse try to meet the challenge of loving again in your post-affair marriage.

"Starting each day I shall remember to communicate my joy as well as my despair so that we can know each other better. Starting each day I shall remind myself to really listen to you and to try to hear your point of view, and discover the least threatening way of giving you mine, remembering that we're both growing and changing in a hundred different ways. Starting each day I shall remind myself that I am a human being and not demand perfection of you until I am perfect. . . . Starting each day I shall remind myself to reach out and touch you gently, with my fingers. Because I don't want to miss feeling you. Starting each day I shall dedicate myself again to the process of being a lover, and then see what happens."

The continued existence of a love relationship, satisfying and exciting to both partners in the post-affair marriage, is no accident. It involves becoming aware of your needs, of what you want in your relationship, and of letting your spouse know in a caring way. It requires that you let him know what statements and actions hurt your feelings or make you angry. Loving again also includes being sensitive to your partner's needs and encouraging him to express them. Finally, it means accepting your spouse for what he really is, an imperfect human being like yourself.

Part IV

Surviving

Chapter 9
A New Beginning

"There's a trick to the Graceful Exit. It begins with the vision to recognize when a job, a life stage, a relationship is over—and to let go. It means leaving what's over without denying its validity or its past importance in our lives.

"It involves a sense of future, a belief that every exit line is an entry, that we are moving on, rather than moving out."

— ELLEN GOODMAN, *WASHINGTON POST* WRITER'S GROUP

As you read this chapter, we are aware that you may be at a turning point in your marital life. You may have evaluated your situation carefully and decided that leaving is better than staying. For some of you, the decision to leave has been made by your partner. Regardless of whose decision it was, for most people the idea of "going it alone" churns up some apprehension.

Not surprisingly, research studies show that divorce is a major stressor. The decision to end the marriage marks the beginning of a transition in your life. A member of one of our support groups read somewhere that a transition period is a time of disequilibrium between two stable periods. In a transition, you are trying to get from one point to another. Getting there, like any kind of travel, involves planning and care, and the knowledge that there will probably be some mishaps along the way. Another member said that she imagined it to be something like walking over a hanging rope bridge. "I know I'll make it," she continued, "if I take it carefully, one step at a time and hold on tight, so as not to let any of the shakes throw me. I have to believe I can do it, and I will."

Recovery from Divorce

Divorce doesn't happen overnight, or when an official document has been handed to you. It is a process. It happens as you work through the difficult feelings associated with divorce and integrate the event into your life. When this is accomplished you will come through the process with a new sense of identity. We believe recovery from divorce takes place in three stages. As we describe them more fully, you will see that the stages of grief discussed in Chapter 4 are part of this process.

First is the denial stage. Denial is a way of protecting yourself from the pain of loss by not recognizing or acknowledging what is occurring. An example of this is the wife who is "the last to know." Once, in a group discussion on this topic, Leo said, "I am not denying anything. She had an affair, and she left me for him. I know it, but I can handle it. It's no big deal. It's a piece of cake."

Leo was not denying what happened, but he was using a kind of denial called "minimizing." Someone who is minimizing may seem very cavalier about the separation. Minimizing is our way of defending against the potential for pain by believing that the situation can be integrated into our lives with a minimum of trouble. Denial says it didn't happen; minimizing says it happened but it doesn't matter. Eventually the denial ends and the magnitude of what has occurred is understood.

Then the second phase, which we call the acute stage, begins. The feeling of disbelief ("I can't believe this is happening") keeps returning, but essentially this stage is characterized by fear, anger, obsessions, restlessness, and attempts to bargain back to better days. In addition, there may be health problems from stress-related illnesses. There is depression, and one's self-esteem is low. Changes in sleeping and eating habits arise, and there is often weight loss. This is a stage of severe distress.

Leah described this stage: "After he told me he was leaving, I became numb. I stayed in bed for days. My oldest daughter ran the house and took care of her brother. Finally I got up and slowly pulled myself together."

The third and last phase in the divorce process is the integration stage. This is characterized by attempts to make changes that are in keeping with the new life events. At this point you will be trying out new behaviors that will help redefine your life and that are necessary for the successful completion of the process. Some find a new career, volunteer, take classes, develop a hobby, get involved in community activities, make new friends, and, in general, begin to take an interest in the world around them. This is a very important juncture and starts the upward path to recovery.

The integration stage is completed when there is an emotional acceptance of the divorce. This is different from the completion of the denial stage, in which acceptance is intellectual. This means that the difficult job of emotional detachment has been accomplished, and a new identity is assumed. The divorce is now part of your history, and you will move forward to meet new goals.

There are times in our group when individuals tell us they are not in any of the stages. Actually, when they think about it, they see that they experienced these feelings at an earlier point. The process for them began after they realized they were unhappy in their marriage and had no hope of it changing. The loss of this desired dream of marriage is a bereavement, and when they thought about it they remembered periods of denial and minimization, followed by other emotions associated with grief.

With infidelity, it is usually the faithful spouse who is at the beginning of the process, while your partner seems further along the way. You may complain that he is very cold and feels no emotion. This is because he has already traveled that rocky road of emotions on which you are just starting. Of course, the reality of it for you is that you must deal not only with the grief process but also the aftermath of the affair. You must also adjust to all the changes that are part of the separation.

This is a period when you may experience a wide array of feelings. Some people are surprised to find that along with apprehension, fear, or panic, they are actually feeling a sense of relief.

As Norman, a former client, said, "I was surprised to feel that a burden had been lifted from my shoulders, but going on without her was terrifying. As bad as our marriage has been, I knew she was going to be there. It's hard to imagine my life in a different way."

For Norman to work through his fears, he had to recognize these feelings without becoming overwhelmed by them. As with all anxieties, he needed to get some emotional distance, calm himself, and change his negative self-talk.

The Triple S Cluster

In years of leading divorce recovery groups, we have found that the most troubling issues fall into the categories relating to survival, social world, and self-esteem. We have called these the Triple S Cluster.

Concerns about survival center on "making it" without the other partner. Each worries about how to handle the responsibilities the other took on. To some it feels like losing a back-up system. In households in which duties were divided in the traditional manner, men often worry about cooking and laundry, women about car and house maintenance. The picture becomes more complicated when there are children in the family. Most single mothers bear almost unrelenting responsibility for child care in addition to work overload. Dawn to dusk responsibility for children, under the best of circumstances, is difficult. Compounded by the changes brought on by separation, coping becomes a monumental task.

As Debra put it, "I am up at six in the morning, getting them off to school and me to work, trying to maintain my professionalism. Then it's back home to make dinner, supervise homework, and baths. Who does the yard work, the housework, and shopping? And who gets up in the middle of the night when the kids are sick? Me. I do it all. I do discipline; he does Disneyland."

Dads see it differently. They feel that they have less influence with their children because they are not with them all the time. Moving away from their home, they feel isolated and not part of their children's everyday lives. Visitation often feels like an artificial way to be with the kids. As Guy told the group, "It's always an arrangement. I worry about where I should take them. It feels unnatural."

Financial worries are a major concern for most couples. More and more we hear women expressing the fear of becoming a bag lady. For most people the income is not enough to sustain the same lifestyle as before. Studies show that the financial status of women drops dramatically after divorce. While many men have financial difficulties after divorce, studies show that most have a higher income within a year.

The second area in the Triple S Cluster has to do with self-esteem. Self-esteem is the way you feel and think about yourself. Although it may drop while you are going through the transition, when it is over, your self-esteem can rise to an even higher level. The dip in the way you feel about yourself will start its upward course as you try new options. Life becomes meaningful once again, and your faith in yourself will be restored. When this occurs you will have developed a new and comfortable identity. Then you will know that you have successfully negotiated this transition.

The last area of this cluster involves your social world. The news of your separation will shake the equilibrium of your relationships with friends and family, like a mobile that was once peaceful but has now been disturbed. Your social network, like those of most others, probably consists of friends, relatives, social acquaintances, work associates, and neighbors—to name a few. As you move through the process of divorce, there will be changes in this network. Some changes you will make; others will be made for you. Some reactions will likely hurt and shock you. As certain friends unexpectedly shy away from you, you may feel abandoned. One of the characteristics of transitions is loss. The loss in the case of divorce involves that of a dream, a role, and a way of thinking about yourself. This includes your circle of friends, which is another way you define yourself. Single women usually feel that they no longer fit in with the world of couples with whom they previously socialized.

One client, Cathy, told us, "It's like I suddenly have some kind of a disease because I'm not part of a couple any more. If I don't have Brent, I am not wanted. I need support and friendship, but they aren't there. It's a couple's world, and I feel very much alone."

Interactions with relatives can be complicated by family loyalties. Stella, a former client, told us that she still considered herself a part of her husband's family. She had expected that being the mother of the children conferred a lasting relationship with Tony's family. She sadly discovered that that status was no longer hers when Tony brought home the other woman. There was a shift in family relations to accommodate the new situation. Boundaries in families change. Relatives who seem like friends may no longer be able to maintain that closeness. Redefining family relationships is often not without tears and sadness.

Feeling as though you no longer fit in is not something you are imagining—it is true. The fact that you are getting a divorce defines you differently to some members in your social network. The role you have played with them is changing, and this is reflected in their interactions with you.

Although at this point you may feel like throwing up your hands in defeat, we ask you to hang in there. The men and women we have counseled feel they have changed in a positive way. Most of them say they have made a better and more satisfying life. Additionally, they have come out of the process feeling good about themselves. We have listed the concerns of others so that you would know you are not alone in what you are feeling, and because we want to offer some help in coping with them.

Taking Care of Yourself

Taking care of yourself during this transition period must become a priority. It is important for you to meet your needs and treat yourself with kindness and consideration on a daily basis. We call this self-nurturing behavior.

Taking care of yourself includes reducing the overload of work and concerns. Professionals can help you. Many women and men have told us they have benefited from working with a therapist, lawyer, financial adviser, real estate agent, or divorce mediator.

As Lionel explained, "There were too many important decisions to be made when all I could do was think about the affair. Somehow, I pulled myself together at work, but at home I couldn't concentrate. When I started therapy and found a real estate agent and financial planner, I felt I was getting some control back in my life."

Babs responded that she felt the same way about the household responsibilities. Until she started a priority list rather than a "wish list" of what she wanted done, she felt exhausted. "But I did some other things too. I hired help for some chores, and started delegating some of the work to the kids. I had felt the work was my responsibility and hesitated to involve the children. That was wrong, I see now. I think it helped them to know that they had to pitch in."

Sorting through the issues and coping with your emotions is often helped by working with a therapist or being in a divorce recovery support group. It is also important to utilize the cognitive approach previously discussed to help combat your negative thinking.

Other ways to nurture yourself are by doing things that bring you pleasure. Some people find it helpful to walk or exercise, meditate, listen to relaxing music, take a bubble bath, keep a daily journal of thoughts and feelings, or pray. As our client Iris put it, "It means that no matter how crummy I feel, I must do something just for myself every day."

Social Support

When you have reached a point where your emotions are not quite so raw, somewhere in the acute stage, you will be ready for a support group. We never cease to be amazed at the degree of caring and support demonstrated in divorce recovery groups. As Marilyn put it, "It really is a 'bridge over troubled waters.' I look forward to Wednesday evenings with friends who understand how I feel."

You may be wondering what happens in such a group. "Will I have to tell the reasons for the divorce or go over the details of the affair?" "Do I have to deal with my unhappy childhood?" The answer to all of these questions is "no."

In a divorce recovery group you will learn ways to understand and cope with your emotions in a safe environment, and you will discuss current issues such as loss, anger, depression, time management, children, and the legal and financial aspects of divorce.

Our client Chloe expressed feelings typical of most participants when she said, "I was really frightened before the first meeting. At that time I had no idea these people would become such an important part of my life. I guess the biggest surprise was that we even laughed in these meetings."

You will find that some group members seem less stressed and appear more able to cope with the situation. But they will tell you that once they felt devastated and immobilized, just as you may be feeling. This is one of the ways in which people are helped in a group. Some members can see how far they have come, while others gain hope that it is possible to feel good again.

You may need to do some investigative work to find a divorce recovery group in your community. Some of the places to check are social service agencies, churches, synagogues, and adult education programs. We suggest speaking with the leader before you attend to determine whether your expectations of the group are appropriate, and whether this is a good time for you to become a member.

New Traditions

In our group one evening, Kenneth said, "I couldn't control her leaving me, but, damn it, I do have something to say about how I'll take it." Research has shown that people like Kenneth, who believe they can control the way an event affects their lives, suffer less from depression than those who perceive themselves as victims. You have probably known of two people who have faced similar circumstances and reacted differently. How can the same event produce different results? To a large extent, it is the way you choose to think about what happens to you that determines how you feel about it. This is not to deny the pain and bereavement that accompanies the end of a marriage. That suffering is very real, but distorted thinking can make the pain worse and make recovering an even more difficult process.

To understand how our thinking affects our emotions and our actions, let's look at what Roxanne told her group one evening. Tearfully she said, "Christmas went down the drain with the marriage." Roxanne's negative thinking will perpetuate the initial feelings of despair and keep her from taking effective action to help herself. By giving in to the belief that she is helpless, she writes Christmas off as another loss. This negative expectation can become a self-fulfilling prophecy.

Roxanne's story brings to mind the solution Kathleen found to a similar predicament. Kathleen was a fifty-one-year-old teacher who had been married for thirty years and who had seven grown children and four grandchildren. Traditionally, Christmas was celebrated at her house with a tree-trimming party and a big family dinner. It was the second Christmas after her divorce, and she approached the holiday with dread, she told the group.

"Last year it was a horror," she said. "The house was empty. I was lonely and depressed. I just waited for the kids to visit. Some did, and some didn't. I can't go through that again. The credit union is offering a trip to Mexico, and some of the other teachers who are going want me to join them. I've never seen Mexico, but that wouldn't seem like Christmas."

The group encouraged her to go. They helped her look at Christmas differently. On her return, she had a New Year's Day brunch for her family, and they all came. Kathleen had a wonderful time. During a follow-up call to her five years later, she said she was still taking the credit union holiday trip and holding the family brunch. "I love it," she said. "Every year at that time I am always mentally thanking the group for encouraging me to make what I had thought was such a radical decision." Although it seemed "radical" at that time, what Kathleen did, and what we hope others will do, is to create a new tradition.

Many cherished traditions change or are no longer workable when a marriage ends. We do not deny the suffering that this brings, but we suggest you can gain some relief from the pain by taking control of lonely weekends, anniversaries, and holidays. Try participating on a regular basis in church activities, charitable organizations, or groups like the Sierra Club that organize weekend or holiday events. Making plans and following through on them can help you regain control of your life. Being proactive is an effective coping strategy for combating depression.

Loneliness

When you are separated, loneliness is a major concern. We have found that when most people are asked what they fear about loneliness, their thinking is irrational on the subject. Like them, you may find it is often your self-talk about being alone that is causing your anxiety more than anything else.

We often hear clients say that being alone means something is wrong with them. By using your cognitive skills, you can challenge some of those self-defeating thoughts. We suggest clients change their self-statements to reflect the fact that they are alone through circumstances, not because something is wrong with them. It is an opportunity to be with yourself.

Sometimes the fear of being alone can be helped by the use of relaxation techniques and through a process of gradual exposure. The way this works is that every time you successfully get through a difficult period of being alone, you will feel stronger and better able to cope the next time.

Our client Rachel put it well when she told the group, "I no longer panic when I am alone the way I did after Neil left me. I do all the things I can to calm myself, and I manage those feelings. It makes me feel better about myself to know that I don't give into the fear. And now there are fewer of these frightening times."

Eventually you may be surprised to find yourself cherishing your time alone. Members of our support groups have reported seeing advantages they had not previously considered. As Alice said, "I never thought I'd say this, but I like the freedom to do what I want when I want. I appreciate having the time to develop or indulge in hobbies and interests."

Emotional loneliness comes from not having an intimate connection to another. One does not necessarily need a mate to satisfy this need. Many marriage partners are unable to achieve an intimate relationship. By intimacy, we mean the ability to listen, share, be empathic, and accept another person regardless of his faults. This kind of closeness can be obtained from friends, relatives, and support groups.

Social isolation is another type of loneliness. Separated and divorced individuals are at risk for this kind of loneliness because of the loss of friendships and the natural tendency to isolate oneself when depressed. Our experience has shown that divorce recovery groups can be the best medicine for social loneliness. It is also important to maintain contact with all other systems of support.

We suggest you maintain contacts with friends through calling, writing, and inviting them to visit. Clients tell us how much a visit from friends or a telephone call can alter a blue mood. Tell people about your marital separation, and if you receive an offer of support, take it! Be sure to contact your supports when you are feeling sad. Members of divorce recovery groups usually exchange phone numbers and provide this support for one another. If no one is available, be sure you have your community hotline number.

Another way to combat loneliness is to find ways to enjoy the time when you are alone. We remember our client Natalie saying, "When I am alone, I've started to think of being *with* myself, not *by* myself. This changed my view of things." What Natalie did was to change her self-talk so that she interpreted her situation differently. Now she spends her time developing her interests.

Some of the activities our clients enjoy are listening to music, gardening, woodworking, reading, sewing, or working out. You probably have more ideas of your own. It is important to be prepared for time alone. You need to have materials available for the woodworking project, the book to read, or the pattern to sew. It's like money in the bank for that rainy day; it's there for you when you need it.

Another way of taking care of yourself is by knowing what triggers a blue mood. If dinner time, Sunday afternoon, or Saturday nights are triggers, then you can prepare for those times. Indicators of dark moods are different for each of us. Some may be compulsive eating, drinking, crying spells, or aimlessly staring into space. Consider these behaviors to be much like a TV channel that you do not want to watch. Switch channels by calling a friend, going for a walk, starting that woodworking project, or distracting yourself by getting out of the house.

Suggesting that you do things by yourself always leads to a major discussion in our support groups. We hear the same responses over and over again:

"The joy of doing is in the sharing."

"Why should I go to a movie if I don't have anyone to discuss it with?"

"If I went to a movie alone, it wouldn't be any fun because everybody would stare at me and wonder why I was alone."

"If I go to a restaurant alone, I'll feel uncomfortable because everyone will be feeling sorry for me for being by myself."

It is usually at this point in our work with clients that we introduce them to Dr. David Burns's book, *Intimate Connections*, in which he discusses pleasure prediction. Dr. Burns believes that people will not participate in certain activities because they decide in advance that it won't be satisfying if they do it alone. This, as you probably have guessed by now, is a thinking distortion. The cure is a three-step process. First, you predict how much pleasure you will get by doing some activity alone; secondly, force yourself to do it; and thirdly, rate your pleasure. Members of our group usually find that they have underestimated how much satisfaction they can get even if they are alone. When our clients are further along the process, we ask them to expand their pleasurable activities to include travel, giving dinner parties, dancing, and other social activities.

If you are a woman, you may feel concerned, like many of the women we have counseled, about the safety issues of being alone. Rather than continue to feel helpless and vulnerable, we suggest that you gather information on ways to make your life safer. In our support groups, we often invite a police officer from the Crime Prevention Unit to talk about personal and home safety issues. In some communities police officers from these units make security inspections of homes. Some members of our group have called in locksmiths to check their homes, while others, for peace of mind, have hired home security companies.

Another concern about being alone that we often hear from divorcing women and men is how to get help in special situations and emergencies.

Try to find someone to share in a mutual help arrangement with you. You will have a sense of security knowing that you can call on someone to drive you to and from the hospital for outpatient surgery, pick you up if your car breaks down, or help if there is a middle-of-the-night emergency call. This means making an agreement with a friend in advance. We have found participants in our support groups respond to each other very positively to help in these situations.

Emotional Detachment

The hallmark of having bridged this transition is the ability to emotionally detach from your spouse. This is not easy to do. As members of our support group report,

"I saw Shirley tonight when I picked up my clean clothes and left the dirty ones."

"Ginger may have left me for him, but she comes to the house every day to cook dinner and clean for us."

"Al's coming over tomorrow to do the bills and paperwork."

"When I came home today, I saw George had stopped by to mow the lawn and paint the railing."

Such attentive behavior is confusing to the spouse, who often interprets it as a sign of ambivalence about leaving the marriage. Our experience has shown that these are indicators of how hard it is to detach.

This attentive behavior becomes the hook that makes it even harder for you to detach, and you find yourself caught in an unfortunate cycle. At this juncture, we recommend clear and explicit communication to clarify the situation, rather than maintaining false hope for a reconciliation.

One of our group members, Juliet, told us that after feeling as though she were on an emotional roller coaster ride, she finally confronted her husband, Ira, by saying "When you call and speak to me for hours on the phone, I believe you still care and want to work on our marriage. I need to know if this is true."

When Ira told her it was not the case, Juliet took a major step toward emotional detachment and said, "I will no longer chat with you on the phone for hours. I will talk to you briefly when we have to attend to business issues, or if we have to discuss something concerning the children." This was difficult for Juliet to say. She realized that she could not recover and get on with her life when she was so tied into these calls with Ira.

First, you must be willing to minimize contact with your spouse, even if it means doing the chores yourself or hiring help. The second step to take is investing in yourself. This means letting go of the obsession with your spouse and focusing on self-nurturing. It won't be easy at first, but in time you may find that, like the members of our support group, you will be happier.

Children

Although divorce is an action taken by parents, it is one that deeply affects children. The degree to which a child is affected depends on many factors, such as the child's developmental stage and gender, other family events and circumstances, and the attitude of the parents. Successful outcomes occur more often in families where parents cooperate and act in the best interests of the children.

The first act of cooperation can come in the manner in which children are told of their parents' decision to divorce. They should be told jointly by both parents and without hostility and anger. This is not the time to put children in the middle of your conflict by telling them of the affair. To do this will raise the children's fears even more. Anxiety is held in check better when the leadership of the family stays calm. The news of a divorce may come as a shock to children, even though they have witnessed parental arguments repeatedly.

There are assurances that you can give your children at this time and throughout the process that will be helpful. They need to know they are not responsible for the separation. Many children feel their misbehavior may have caused the break-up. Children may start to bargain, vowing to behave better if Daddy will stay. They must be reassured that their behavior had nothing to do with your decision, and there isn't anything they can do to change your mind. Children will try to talk parents out of the decision and even scheme at ways to bring about a reconciliation. It is best to be firm but kind at this point by telling them that it is the parents' decision, and they cannot change it. Rather than giving them false hope, you must gently make them aware of the permanence of the situation.

Some children become worried when they hear that their parents no longer love each other. They become frightened that Mommy and Daddy may also stop loving them. You can help them by explaining how parental love is different and that you will not stop loving them.

Children's anxieties can be reduced by giving them concrete information. They want to know where they will live, where they will go to school, and when they will see the noncustodial parent, their grandparents, and their cousins. One child told us she was afraid that her mother and she would meet her father in the supermarket, and her parents wouldn't speak to each other. Another was afraid that his father would no longer come to see him play soccer.

To the extent that you can minimize disruption in their daily lives, you will be supporting them at this difficult time. Children thrive on routine and stability. If you ask them to take sides, carry messages, or become confidants, you are placing them in the middle of adult issues. This behavior can put them at risk for emotional problems. One mother told us that after her son's visitation with his father, he came home with a bouquet for her from her ex-husband and a demand to know why she was so mean to Daddy.

Children are conflicted by issues of loyalty. You have probably seen this with friends as well and realize how confused adults can become. The confusion is even greater for children. One of the best gifts that you can give your child at this point is permission to love and enjoy the relationship with your former spouse and his family.

An affair also affects children. Loyalty issues surface for them when they are aware that a parent is having a relationship with someone else. Children often feel that they are caught in the middle. For example, if Dad is having the affair, it is possible for the child to be caught in a triangle with Mom and the other woman.

You can keep them out of adult conflicts by not speaking badly of your spouse and the other woman and by continuing to set your usual standards of behavior.

As Gail tearfully told us, "It was so hard to send the kids off with their father and Irene. I wanted to call Irene every name in the book, but instead I instructed them on being polite and doing what they were told. They knew when they left the house that I expected them to treat Irene with the respect they were taught to show all adults."

Although it was hard for Gail to restrain herself, she was able to rise above her own urge to retaliate and to do her part to keep the children out of a triangle. Gail had to fight the feeling that she was sending her children off to another mother. It is important to recognize that this is emotional reasoning, a thinking distortion. The third person is a new individual with whom your children have to establish a relationship. They need your help at this time. By managing your anxiety and inspiring them by your example, your children will be better prepared to cope with this difficult adjustment.

Guidelines for Helping Your Children

1. Children should be told of the decision jointly by both parents without hostility and anger.

2. They should not be put in the middle of adult conflicts by telling them of the affair.

3. Children need to know they are not responsible for the break up of the marriage.

4. Children should be told that it is the parents' decision, and they cannot change it.

5. Children need to know their parents still love them even though they no longer love each other.

6. Children should be given concrete information about how their lives will change.

7. You should listen to children's concerns, and try to minimize disruption in their daily lives.

8. Children should not be asked to take sides, carry messages, or become your confidants.

9. Children should be given permission to love and enjoy the relationship with your former spouse and his family. Try to find positive things to say about them.

Moving Forward

One way that you can move forward and close the door on the pain of the affair and the end of your marriage is by creating a ritual for yourself. We discussed rituals and how they can be used for healing. We saw this in a support group when our client Felicia told us how she had wanted to date, yet felt uncomfortable about it. One day she thought of taking her wedding band and placing it on a ribbon, which she tied around some flowers she had picked from her garden.

"I asked my children, who are eleven and thirteen, to watch. I spoke of my sad feelings about the marriage ending, the good memories we would always cherish, and my delight at the wonderful children that the marriage produced. I talked about the future my ex-husband and I shared around the children, but I also spoke about my need to move on and to create another future for myself. Then I put the flowers in a box and placed them in the attic. Now I feel ready to date, and I believe my children will be more able to accept it," she concluded.

There is a certain sadness we feel in endings to any period in our lives. We remember the dreams of the beginning and the joys of happier days along with the disappointments and heartaches. But an ending means a new beginning, and with it a promise of what could be. We want to help you look forward to new dreams of the future with a sense of well-being about yourself, knowing that your self-esteem is intact and your faith in yourself is strong.

Chapter 10

Increasing Your Self-Esteem

"I know there are aspects about myself that
puzzle me, and other aspects that I do not know.
But as long as I am friendly and loving to
myself, I can courageously and hopefully look
for the solutions to the puzzles and for ways to
find out more about me. I own me, and therefore,
I can engineer me. I am me and I am okay."

— *PEOPLEMAKING*, VIRGINIA SATIR

One evening during a group discussion on infidelity, a remark by our member Hal generated much discussion about self-esteem. Hal said, "I was surprised at how badly I felt about myself after she had the affair. I really was down on myself. I felt this way at work, with other people, and I wondered whether anything I ever did was any good."

Leslie, another member, quickly responded, "I know what you mean. I've been feeling lousy. I hate him and, at the same time, I have lost faith in myself and my ability to trust. It all boils down to self-esteem. I have lost it, if I've ever even had it. I guess that's the bottom line."

You may be having similar thoughts. One of our goals in writing *Surviving Infidelity* is to help you come through this experience with positive self-esteem. Self-esteem is the sum of the way we evaluate ourselves and, as Leslie believes, is crucial to our lives.

The choices we make in life are influenced by our self-esteem. So are our reactions to events, such as infidelity, and, in general, the satisfaction we experience in life. Self-esteem is not only a factor in determining one's choice of mate, it continues to influence that relationship and, in turn, be influenced by it. We know that self-esteem affects almost every aspect of our lives and can change according to what is happening to us.

Divorce and infidelity adversely affect the way we feel about ourselves. This is true even for those whose feelings about themselves are basically positive. Although self-esteem drops during life transitions, it can return to previous levels or rise to even higher ones.

Joan, a former client, said, "My friend Alma thinks well of herself, and that's how I want to be. She is considerate of others, but yet, she doesn't ignore her own needs to please everyone, the way I do. I am always looking for everyone's approval. I want to appreciate what I do even if no one else notices it. I want my own approval to be the one that counts. I know I brought this need into my marriage. My husband told me that he is taking responsibility for the affair, but I am going to own up to this exaggerated need for approval."

Self-Esteem and Infidelity

Self-esteem is a factor in determining the kind of person you are attracted to and choose to marry. When people marry with the idea that marriage will improve their self-esteem, they are on shaky ground. For example, Glenda, a former client, married Evan in order to be taken care of, believing herself to be less capable than others and in need of protection in a complex world. Essentially, Glenda used marriage to try to solve her problem of low self-esteem. Evan soon felt overburdened by Glenda's dependency and sought a solution in an affair. This affair occurred because of unfulfilled expectations.

Affairs are more likely to happen during a life transition. When personal problems and basic deficits in self-esteem are not resolved but only kept at bay, the marriage can then be further strained by a transition such as a death in the family, retirement, or a loss of health or status. Such families may be more at risk for an affair.

Affairs at midlife or at retirement age may also be attempts to deal with self-esteem concerns. For example, someone who thinks he is growing old and is not satisfied with how he has dealt with his life may try to ward off those feelings with an affair.

Low self-esteem is often the reason some individuals repeatedly find themselves in situations that show a lack of commitment. In marriages we see it in a fear of intimacy played out in affairs as happens with the serial lover. You must have a good sense of self-worth to be able to open up and share intimate aspects of yourself with another. Our client Frank, whose troubled childhood accounted for his low opinion of himself, told us, "It was just easier to laugh, flirt, and have one-night-stands than to spend quiet evenings at home sharing with Delores."

When self-esteem is a factor in an affair, it must be addressed. Enhancing the way you feel about yourself will be important regardless of the outcome of this crisis. If you are working on a reconciliation, your attention to self-esteem issues is necessary so that they will not again upset the stability of the marriage.

Enhancing Self-Esteem

Although as a child you may not have had the skills to combat situations that were damaging to your feelings of self-worth, as an adult the situation is different. You can now be responsible for taking care of yourself and learning new ways to build and enhance your self-esteem. We would like to explore ways you can do this. The following list can guide you as you work toward that goal.

1. Recognize and challenge childhood messages that were discouraging and negatively affected your self-esteem.
2. Recognize and challenge societal messages that are damaging to your self-esteem.
3. Recognize and refute any thinking distortions you use that maintain low levels of self-esteem.
4. Recognize and refute put-downs by others that are damaging to your self-esteem.
5. Recognize and assert your personal rights.
6. Recognize that many factors are operating in families, so that you can free yourself of inappropriate blame and guilt.
7. Make taking care of yourself a priority.

Developing Self-Esteem

Because self-esteem is a basic factor in determining our choices and interpretations of events, it is helpful to understand its development. Alfred Adler, a psychiatrist and early contributor to the field of personality theory, was concerned with the development of self-esteem. His concepts can help you challenge any negative childhood messages that may be affecting your adult relationships.

When you grow up in a family atmosphere of encouragement, you are likely to develop high levels of self-esteem and a belief in your own resourcefulness. On the other hand, if you are raised with discouragement, you arc apt to give up on yourself and develop self-defeating ways of thinking and behaving. A child who is discouraged about himself in areas his parents value may grow up feeling that he doesn't measure up.

Hank described this to us one day in a group, "I was the youngest in a very athletic family. Sports were everything. I didn't do well at them and found that I'd rather read. My father and brothers teased me and were always on my case. By today's standards, I would be called a nerd. Even though I do well on my job, I still think it's a fluke and that I am not any good.

"I am now seeing how this affected my marriage," continued Hank. "Whenever my wife disagreed with me, I exaggerated the meaning of what she said and felt criticized. I tried to please her to the point of losing who I was. Time has passed since I was so ridiculed as a child, but I guess those feelings are still with me."

Adler also noted that sometimes children are assigned roles, such as the good little girl or the bad boy. This influences the way they feel about themselves. A child growing up with encouragement and freedom to choose his role will have a better chance of developing high self-esteem than one brought up with blaming and labeling.

Low self-esteem can result in personal problems, flawed interpersonal relationships, depressed moods, and self-defeating attempts at solving problems. This may show up in various ways, like marrying the wrong person for the wrong reasons or having one or more affairs.

Based on their interpretations of family experiences, people often make mistaken assumptions that become the core of what they think of themselves, the world, and what they must do to survive. An example of such thinking is, "I am incompetent, the world is dangerous, and therefore I need someone to take care of me."

People continue to make errors in thinking by interpreting things that happen to them in a way that confirms these beliefs. In this way, a woman who believes herself to be unattractive may decide that her husband's affair is the result of her appearance. Such an assumption could keep her from looking at the issues in her life or marriage and continue to keep her self-esteem low. Such thinking errors come from childhood messages that prevent you from growing up with pride in yourself. You can change them by recognizing and challenging them.

Challenging Childhood Messages

A first step in rebuilding self-esteem is to think about the family messages you grew up believing. Decide what messages need to be challenged and use your knowledge of thinking errors to do so. In Feeling Good, Dr. David Burns says that self-esteem exists when you "are not arbitrarily haranguing and abusing yourself, but choose to fight back against those automatic thoughts with meaningful rational responses."

Let's take an example of how this works. Gerry, a forty-one-year-old woman in one of our support groups, said of her marriage, "I thought I was very lucky that Richard wanted to marry me in the first place. I never had anything interesting to say. My mother always said that I was like a bump on a log. My sister was the life of the party and that was what Richard was like. I'd go out and everybody would expect you to just join in and be part of the festivities. Richard could do that for me—just like my sister did. When I was with them, no one noticed that I was just a bump on a log. Even I can understand why Richard had an affair."

Gerry had little awareness or appreciation of her own abilities. She accepted someone else's definition of who she was. In her last statement, she even defended this definition by suggesting that her husband's infidelity was caused by her being dull. Using our understanding of thinking distortions, we can see that Gerry minimized her good qualities, jumped to conclusions about the reason for the affair, and labeled herself. The group helped her do some reality checking from what they saw and knew of her. They challenged her conclusion about the affair and asked her whether she could be using it as an excuse to keep her and Richard from working on the marriage.

You can further challenge negative messages by substituting positive statements for them. These new statements are called positive affirmations. Gerry could substitute a new statement for the negative one, "I never have anything interesting to say." Her new statement becomes, "I am worth listening to." Positive affirmations need to be repeated just as negative messages were until they become a part of your thinking.

Negative Belief	Positive Affirmation
You can't do anything right.	I make contributions to our family life.
Nobody likes you.	I am a good friend and I have loyal friends.
I am no bargain.	I have many assets of which I am proud.

Society's Messages

Messages from early childhood are not the only ones that influence the way we come to think about ourselves. Society's values and judgments have considerable impact upon our self-esteem. Just as the family can send out messages of discouragement, so can society. Its messages to those whose spouses have been unfaithful can be very discouraging, and sometimes blaming.

For example, Carrie said to the group one evening, "When I told my neighbor about Clifford's affair, she commented, 'What did you expect? You have varicose veins and stretch marks. Why should he want to sleep with you when he can run his hand down some smooth firm body?' It hurt like hell to hear another woman was more desirable to him. I can't compete with someone twelve years younger."

Carrie's neighbor jumped to conclusions about the affair, labeled Carrie, and ignored the possibility that she couldn't and didn't know the facts. Carrie bought into her neighbor's thinking that her husband had an affair because she wasn't sexy enough. This is a message both men and women hear repeatedly from movies and TV.

The most prevalent societal judgment about infidelity is that you failed your mate sexually, causing him to look elsewhere. This assumption is made because affairs are sexual. However, most affairs do not occur primarily for sex. Affairs are barometers of trouble elsewhere—in the individual, the relationship, or both.

Other women report that they have been accused of not making their spouse happy. When we suggest, in our groups, that each person is responsible for his own happiness and not that of the other, the idea is met with great resistance. We do not deny that one of the purposes of marriage is to be happy. In fact, in a self-esteem support group, on a sentence completion exercise that began with, "When I got married, I believed . . ." almost all of the responses were, "I'd live happily ever after."

Couples do work together to be happy with each other, but this is different from making another person responsible for your happiness. The responsibility couples have to each other is to be respectful and supportive. If you are unhappy, you can compromise and resolve differences, improve communication with your mate, and work on marital problems.

In one group, Madeleine, a middle-aged woman with grown children, told the group how angry she had been on Saturday mornings when her husband napped on the sofa. She wanted him to meet her expectations of getting out for lunch, driving in the country, or visiting friends. When she started making her own plans and taking responsibility for her own enjoyment, she felt less angry, depressed, and powerless. As the resentment diminished, Madeleine was able to use her communication skills to discuss the situation and make some changes. She and her spouse each had responsibility for creating the situation that brought happiness to their marriage.

Thinking Distortions

Just as it is important to recognize and refute your own thinking distortions, you must speak up when others try to put you down. Insults, for example, are often used in jest.

Let's look at how this works. In a seemingly harmless situation, your friend labels you clumsy when you drop a dish. You say nothing, but you may think of yourself as clumsy, thus confirming a belief about yourself that you can't do anything right. You raise your self-esteem and put an end to the labeling when you say that you are not clumsy; you simply dropped a dish.

In the case of infidelity there are sometimes accusations from family and friends that you have been an inadequate mate or else the affair wouldn't have happened. By refusing to accept the label of inadequate mate, you are letting people know you are a valuable human being and expect to be treated with respect.

In one of our groups, Selina told us her mother blamed her for her husband's affair, saying it was due to her lack of attention to him while she was attending night school. By this time, Selina was well versed in distorted thinking and would not regard herself poorly on the basis of her mother's accusations and told her so. Selina told her mother, "I am not responsible for my husband's actions. I am not to blame. He made his own decisions."

Recognizing and refuting such remarks by family and friends will not only make you feel better about yourself but will increase their respect for you. This requires, however, that you respond to them when you hear putdowns. This may be difficult to do when your self-esteem is low, because you may not believe that you have the right to do it. Therefore, we would like to turn our attention to self-esteem and assertiveness.

Self-Esteem and Assertiveness

People feel much better about themselves when they become more assertive. Assertiveness is the middle ground between two extremes: nonassertiveness and aggressiveness. It communicates two-way respect—

respect for yourself and respect for others. Assertive communication is an open, honest expression of your feelings and opinions in an appropriate fashion. As assertiveness increases, marital relationships and interactions with family and friends improve, as does self-esteem.

However, in our groups, we often hear confusion about assertiveness. For example, one quiet young woman named Sophia said, "I know people take advantage of me, but I would rather that happen than to be like my mother-in-law, who orders everyone around." Neal responded, "Speaking up isn't always the problem. My wife understands what I want. Damn it! I assert myself loud and clear, but I don't see it improving our relationship."

These are examples of extremes in communication. Sophia speaks nonassertively. She acts as though others have rights and she has none. Sophia ends up feeling badly about herself, as if she were a doormat. In these examples, both Neal and Sophia's mother-in-law communicate aggressively. They act as though only they have rights.

Speaking up for yourself shows high self-esteem and, by the same token, is a statement of belief in your personal rights. People with low self-esteem are often surprised to find that they have personal rights. They usually feel that other people are more entitled to be treated with respect than they are. But everyone is entitled to respect.

We would like to share some rights for you to claim as your own. Among them are the right to feel, think, and say what you would like as long as you are considerate of others. Assertiveness includes the right to disagree, choose your friends, make your own decisions, and judge your own behavior. We suggest you form your own list of personal rights. Begin your list with the statement, "I have the right to . . ." and complete the list with as many rights as you can generate.

Now that you are aware of your rights, you will begin to feel better about yourself by acting assertively. As you become more assertive, you will be better able to express your feelings about infidelity, state your needs, and respond to the put-downs of others. After all, it's your right to do so.

Taking Care of Yourself

In a support group one evening when we asked members to share things they enjoyed doing, Florence replied, "There isn't anything I enjoy doing. My whole life was taking care of my husband. I wanted to do what he desired. I was always there for him no matter how I felt. I listened for hours on end to his problems. I really lived for him. And now I have no life."

Florence lived through her spouse and failed to care for herself. She ignored or minimized her own needs in order to be what she considered a good wife. This is an example of the "de-selfing" behavior which we described earlier.

In her book, *Revolution from Within: A Book of Self-Esteem*, Gloria Steinem asks, "If you have a partner, do you spend more time thinking about pleasing and/or improving him than pleasing and/or improving yourself? In general, is your sense of well-being determined more by the state of your love life than by your own life?" If this characterizes your thinking, taking care of yourself must now become a priority for you. It is a way of building self-esteem. You may feel uncomfortable at first while you are changing a long-standing habit, but this discomfort should gradually lessen.

You can begin by finding out who you are. One way to do this is by writing your thoughts in a daily diary. Other ways are by doing activities that bring you pleasure. If you are like our group member Florence, who had completely replaced her own interests with those of her husband, you can give yourself the gift of time to explore community activities and classes for your own pleasure.

In addition, you can increase the pleasantness in your life by creating the physical, social, and spiritual environment that pleases you. Treating yourself well is not selfish behavior, as you may have been taught. Rather it is self-nurturing and vital to your emotional well-being.

Self-Esteem and Family Interactions

Looking at your family's history, roles, values, and significant events will help you better understand yourself and improve your self-esteem. We want to share an exercise with you in which we ask you to stand back and look at your life as though you were viewing a play from a seat in the balcony. Looking from this distance helps you gain a perspective that will promote understanding and remove unnecessary blame and guilt. By doing this exercise, we hope you will come to understand that no one is completely responsible for any one event.

We begin this exercise by asking you to describe the cast of players in this drama of your life. This will include members of both your immediate and extended families. Review their beliefs, behavior, and histories, including all significant events such as births, deaths, and illnesses. Also include their disappointments, like the marriage that never happened, the career that didn't materialize, and the baby that was not conceived. Place your drama in historical time by telling what was happening that affected the lives of the players. Your goal is to help the audience understand what the players are thinking and feeling so that you can better understand the drama.

When our client Adrienne tried this exercise, she realized for the first time how conflicted she was by the messages of her traditional mother and the desires of her husband for a different lifestyle. When her husband lost his job and their daughter was ready to leave home after high school graduation, her husband had an affair.

"I guess," Adrienne continued, "the growing differences between my husband and me came to a head when he lost his job. He became very depressed. I, also, was depressed because our only child left home. I devoted our married life to her. I realized after seeing my own drama from the balcony that we were both dealing with losses and were stressed. I can almost understand his affair, in a way, that is. I am still angry, but not as much as I had been. I also don't blame myself like I did when I first heard about it. This has helped me come to terms with it more than I had. I am not going to be so rigid and I want to change our lifestyle now. I think it will be good for both of us."

Self-Esteem Building Exercises

Self-esteem can be enhanced throughout life. Listed below are some exercises to help you understand some of the roots of your self-esteem and utilize that information in positive ways. The exercises have been arranged so that each builds upon the previous one. Start with the first and try one every three or four days. You will need time between exercises to think about what you have learned and, in some cases, to do a suggested assignment.

Exercise 1

Look at childhood pictures of you and your family. Notice body language. Did members stand close together or apart? What do the facial expressions tell you? Find yourself in the picture and speak to that child with the encouragement he needs to feel good about himself and his abilities to handle himself in the world.

Exercise 2

Think back over your family messages from childhood. It may help you to look at the pictures to remember them. In the second column below, write down some of the messages you received from the people listed in the first column. Study the messages in the second column and, using your knowledge of thinking distortions whenever possible, respond assertively.

Family Member	Message	Response
Father		
Mother		
Brother(s)		
Sister(s)		
Grandparents		
Example		
Father	Things are bad and they are going to get worse.	Things may be bad, but no one knows if they are going to get worse. Dad is jumping to conclusions.

Exercise 3

Using the same directions as in Exercise 2, write what you learned from your family about being:

Topic	Message	Response
Female		
Male		
Competitive		
Married		
Sexual		
Unfaithful		
Example		
Men	It's OK for men to fool around. It's their nature.	It is not OK. This is a choice, not nature.

Exercise 4

Listed below are some beliefs commonly held in today's society. They can all be viewed as thinking errors. Believing in them will most likely affect your self-esteem in a negative way. Use this exercise to respond to those that bother you.

a. It's undignified for older people to have sex.
b. Women over fifty are undesirable.
c. Men shouldn't cry.
d. Men can't talk about feelings.
e. If a man has an affair, something must have been wrong with his wife.
f. It's OK to have a fling as long as it doesn't hurt anybody.
g. What you don't know can't hurt you.

Exercise 5

Think back over your life to a difficult period or episode you feel you handled satisfactorily. List the skills and strengths you used to resolve the situation or that helped you cope.

Example:

When Don was sick, I found strength by not allowing my mind to wander to the worst thing that could happen. I prayed and took long hot baths to relax. When I spoke to the doctor, I was organized and had all the questions written down that I wanted to ask. I spoke up if something happened that upset me.

Exercise 6

Write a paragraph describing yourself for your alumni newsletter.

Exercise 7

Make a list of things you like to do. Place a check next to those items you are not doing. Write the reasons why you are not doing them. Analyze your reasons, refute any thinking errors, and try to put these activities in your life. This is part of taking care of yourself.

Example:

I would like to go out to eat. People will wonder what is wrong with me because I am alone. This is jumping to conclusions. I am mind reading. I don't know what they are thinking. I don't even know if I enter their thoughts at all. Plenty of people are alone, and many go to the movies by themselves. This doesn't mean anything is wrong with them or that people are thinking about them. I will try going to the movies by myself this weekend.

Exercise 8

Imagine the way you want to answer someone who labels you incorrectly. Write out what you would say.

Example:

> You always say that I'm timid and don't have a thought in my mind. Well, that's a label I won't accept. I am quiet around you because you don't listen. So I have stopped talking. I have lots of thoughts in my head, but I've chosen not to share them with you.

Exercise 9: Positive Affirmations

List five positive statements about yourself on two index cards. Leave one on your dresser and carry the second card with you. On rising in the morning and before going to sleep at night, say these five affirmations to yourself three times. At lunch time and at coffee breaks, use the card you carry with you and repeat or read the affirmations to yourself three times. After a month, write new affirmations and repeat the process. Continue doing this until you give up your negative and destructive thinking.

• • •

Although love and marriage can enrich your life and be a source of support in bad times, they are not the answer to surviving hardships and disappointments. The answer comes from you. Within you lie the strength and fortitude to think about yourself differently—as a survivor. With a different set of beliefs you can throw away the role of the victim and with determination become the survivor.

Chapter 11
What It Takes to Be a Survivor

"I am the master of my fate:
I am the captain of my soul."
INVICTUS, R.T. HAMILTON BRUCE

Our goal in this book is to help you survive infidelity and the impact it has on your life and family. Using a cognitive approach, we have emphasized the importance of the power to choose how to think, feel, and act. We have taught skills to help change your thinking that will determine the way you react emotionally.

To round out this picture, we would like to share our ideas about what it takes to be a survivor. The survivors quoted in this chapter have a valuable message for you. Although they have endured very severe situations, these people were able to transcend their experiences and come out strong. They survived the "slings and arrows of outrageous fortune."

What we have learned from those who found themselves in extreme situations can be of help to you in healing the pain of infidelity. Dr. Edith Eger, a psychologist, survivor of Auschwitz, and international lecturer on the Holocaust, said, "The skills that concentration camp survivors used to sustain themselves apply to a broad range of psychological problems. . . . It's not the cancer, the divorce; it's how I go about dealing with it."

The writings of survivors describe circumstances that many would say were too devastating to recover from. Yet these women and men did survive, just as our clients have. Much of what we have learned from them actually becomes a summary of what we have presented already. Listed below are the beliefs and skills needed to survive difficult situations:

- Belief in your own resourcefulness
- Ability to withstand uncomfortable feelings
- Belief in something greater than yourself
- Ability to see the complexity of events

- Ability to view events in a time frame
- Ability to formulate a plan
- Ability to ask for help and support
- Ability to let go of resentment
- Ability to recognize the power of thoughts for healing
- Ability to find meaning in one's experience

Belief in Your Own Resourcefulness

Faith in your own resourcefulness to handle whatever comes your way is, perhaps, the most useful belief in handling adversity. Dr. Edith Eger also said, "What we learned in the concentration camp was self-reliance. We had a choice. We could have let the experience devastate or strengthen us. That's true for everyone."

One of the best examples of this belief came from our client, Claudia, who told us about an exercise in her counseling class. The instructor passed out a series of pictures and asked the students to record their reactions. The first picture was of a barren field with horses grazing in a corner where a small plot of grass still remained. Claudia said to us, "I got very pessimistic. There will be no more grass, and the horses will die. The teacher asked another student for his response, and he said, 'It looks like they are running out of grass. I guess they'll have to move on and find another field.' Well, I was shocked," Claudia went on, "I never thought they could do anything about it. I guess I just give in right away and never think that there may be some alternatives."

Resourcefulness is using your own abilities to find solutions for your problems. In times of stress, we often feel helpless and believe we are powerless to cope. The key to coping is in the way you choose to think about yourself—as a survivor, not a victim. Survivors look at the strengths and skills that helped them in the past and try to apply them to their current situation.

When author Judith Viorst discusses love and mourning in her book *Necessary Losses*, she says that mourning depends in part on "our inner strengths and outer supports, and will surely depend on our past history." *Inner strengths* refers to our attitudes and belief systems, while *past history* includes not only our life events but also our past coping skills.

Ability to Withstand Uncomfortable Feelings

Withstanding uncomfortable feelings at this time is hard to do, because infidelity brings up deep-rooted fears of rejection and abandonment.

Coping means living with such feelings while trying to understand what has happened, resolve the issues raised, and integrate the event into your life. The survivor tries to put the infidelity into perspective rather than becoming overwhelmed and immobilized by anxiety, depression, or anger.

Hillary Rodham Clinton is a perfect example of such a person. The public was aware of the humiliation and pain that her husband's infidelity imposed upon her. Yet she endured these uncomfortable feelings, took a family break with a vacation to Martha's Vineyard, and then resumed her duties as First Lady.

Many of the skills taught in this book will help you through the process of integrating this event into your life. Using your cognitive skills will lessen the anxiety produced by thinking errors, so that you are detached enough to problem solve.

Belief in Something Greater Than Yourself

Being able to see yourself as part of something greater can offer support as you work through pain. Studies show that people with such views suffer less from depression. Such a belief may be spiritual, religious, or philosophical. Martin Luther King, Jr., alluded to the power of his faith when he said, "I have a dream." His dream inspired many who survived those bleak days.

When we watched Rose Kennedy mourn the tragic and violent deaths of her sons, John F. Kennedy and Robert Kennedy, somehow we understood it was her deep religious belief that sustained her through this ordeal.

Members of Alcoholics Anonymous and other twelve-step programs recognize a higher power in helping them overcome alcoholism. The term higher power is left to each individual's interpretation. To some it means God, and to others a spirituality within themselves.

Holocaust literature shows that even through one of the worst ordeals in history, many held on to their beliefs and survived.

In her book *Out of Africa*, writer Isak Dinesen told of her husband's infidelity. She contracted syphilis from him and suffered its effects all her life. She had to endure the harsh medical treatments available at that time; her illness was a constant reminder of his betrayal. Dinesen immersed herself in a dream that meant everything to her. She cultivated a coffee farm in Africa and expended her energies on it in the face of severe financial difficulties.

Being able to see yourself as part of something greater brings hope. This changes the texture and color of your existence, making an adverse situation seem temporary and less desperate. If you are a spiritual or religious person, getting in touch with that aspect of yourself may help you in coping with infidelity and its aftermath.

Ability to See the Complexity of Events

Survivors are able to see the complexity of situations, and they recognize that the factors that determine any event are not as simple as "*A* causes *B*." Completing the drama exercise discussed in the previous chapter helped you to gain an appreciation of the complexity of family interactions. This recognition can change your perspective. If you are feeling upset, you may be able to re-evaluate your emotions. For example, guilt can change to regret, or anxiety to concern. You may still wish that things had turned out differently, but the degree of your reaction can be reduced.

Rabbi Harold Kushner, author of *When Bad Things Happen To Good People*, recounts the tragedy that he and his wife survived when their son, Aaron, was diagnosed as having progeria. This rare childhood disease accelerates the aging process so that the child becomes old and dies within a few years. The rabbi wonders why this should happen to good people like him and his wife and decides it is because of the randomness of the universe. We simply cannot control all the factors or variables in the world or in our lives.

Recognition that some events are beyond our control is an important concept for surviving. For example, the well-known Serenity Prayer used in twelve-step programs encourages participants to ask for help to change that which can be changed, to accept that which cannot be changed, and to have the wisdom to know the difference.

In *To Secure A Safe Passage*, the authors share their wisdom about coming to terms with tragedy. Dr. Pauline Rabin, a psychiatrist, and her husband David wrote this book before David's death. Dr. David Rabin was a brilliant and internationally known physician with Lou Gehrig's disease, a crippling and fatal illness. In the last chapter of the book, David is interviewed by Richard M. Zaner, a philosopher, who comments that David probably wonders, "Why me?" David replies, "Why not me?" He stunned the philosopher with the objectivity of his reply. Amazingly, David had the ability to step outside of his situation. Implied in his answer was that he was not a victim; it could happen to anyone. This is the randomness of the universe.

Survivors of physical, social, or emotional tragedies recognize that many factors are beyond their control. No one can control all the variables of life. We want you to know that the same is true with infidelity.

Ability to View Events in a Time Frame

If you believe that the misery of today will be with you all the time, then you have set yourself up to feel hopelessness and despair. The knowledge that time heals is one of the beliefs that can keep you going through the bad periods. The passage of time allows you to work through your emotions, accept the infidelity, and make the necessary accommodations in your life.

In her courageous and sensitive book *Stronger Than Death*, psychiatrist Susan Chance writes about her recovery after the suicide of her son, an only child. As she shares her deepest thoughts, we come to understand how she developed her survival skills. She quotes from a diary she kept after his death and says, "My belief that time will help, helps me." Because Dr. Chance is so open with her feelings, we can see that survival is not always a smooth journey but one filled with setbacks and moments of doubt.

Ability to Formulate a Plan

When you start thinking of plans, you are taking a major step toward recovery. At the outset, your plans should be narrow in focus and attainable.

Setting such goals was illustrated by our client Jennifer, a forty-four-year-old woman whose twenty-year marriage ended with her husband's marrying the other woman. Reminiscing, Jennifer said, "At first I told myself, 'I only need to get through the next hour. How can I do that?'" Then she added, "I started increasing the time to getting through the morning, then the afternoon, and night. Finally, I got to the one-day-at-a-time stage. It took me months before I could make more concrete plans, like finding a job. I knew I could get there if I did it slowly."

What Jennifer did was tailor her plans to where she was in the process of recovery. It would have been unrealistic for Jennifer to try job hunting when she felt she could only deal with her emotions one hour at a time.

Like many survivors, Jennifer knew time would help her healing, but she needed a plan that would change as she changed. Initial plans for dealing with infidelity must first address the crisis. You may not be able to formulate the plan without help from a therapist, a member of the clergy, or a crisis center. One client, Helene, described it well when she said, "When I first found out that he was involved with another woman, I felt as though I was 'losing it.' It was like being in a hurricane, trying to stand on one foot while you are being battered by strong winds. You just can't do it. You need some help." After the crisis becomes stabilized, you can begin to work on the issue of infidelity in your marriage.

Dr. Abraham Maslow, the psychologist, wrote about the hierarchy of needs. In this order, basic needs must be satisfied before the next can be addressed. The first step in his hierarchy includes essential needs of life such as food, air, and water. We are in a crisis when these needs are not satisfied. This theory is relevant to helping people get organized in a crisis. The first step must include ways to meet these basic life requirements. Then one can move up the hierarchy to satisfy other needs, such as love and self-esteem.

Planning is a healthy sign of recovery because it indicates that your feeling of powerlessness is diminishing. You are no longer feeling as helpless or hopeless as you once did. Your intense emotions are subsiding, and you are moving forward.

Dr. Susan Chance strongly encourages people when she writes that they should take over and make it better for themselves. They have a choice whether to stay stuck in blaming and moaning about all the things that have been unfair or to get on with it and do the best they can with what they have. She goes on to say that nobody likes that message, "but it has the utility of being both true and ultimately helpful."

Ability to Ask for Help and Support

Survivors know that finding support and help during a crisis is crucial. Our experience has shown that women are more likely to look toward other people for support than are men. As evidence, women outnumber men in support groups. Among the possible reasons for this may be that women are traditionally more comfortable expressing feelings and nurturing others. In our groups, male members—most of whom have never experienced this kind of bonding—have been very appreciative of the support received, and they quickly became converts to more intimacy in relationships.

Support, like much of what affects us in life, falls along a continuum. You can ask for help in small to large doses depending on the character of the relationship. For example, in cases of separation and divorce, speaking to your child's teacher and pediatrician to make them aware of what is happening is a way of finding support in small doses. These are people who can offer support appropriate to their relationship with you.

Further along the continuum may be neighbors, friends who share a special interest, or coworkers. Although you may not consider your relationships with them to be close, their understanding can provide support.

At the end of the continuum are close friends who are willing to listen. Not all of them can fulfill this need for support, and some can do so only for limited amounts of time. Checking it out by directly asking your friend whether he can spare some listening time is the best way for you to know. Many people are surprised to find that support can come from new acquaintances, such as those you meet in support groups. Looking for support on a continuum is an important and guiding concept, giving you more options and making it easier to look in a variety of places.

Ability to Let Go of Resentment

Resentment is like a prisoner's shackles, keeping you in one place and taking away your freedom. The survivor realizes that resentment is a major block to personal serenity. Hurt that is allowed to grow festers and results in bitterness and time lost in suffering. Earlier we wrote of Betty Broderick, who murdered her husband and his second wife, "the other woman." Broderick could not let go of her resentment and get on with her life. She is figuratively and literally a prisoner and has missed out on the daily pleasure of being with her children and enjoying freedom.

Accepting infidelity as part of your marriage is not the same as condoning it. Infidelity occurred. This cannot be changed. But allowing yourself to obsess over it and label it as the worst thing that could have happened gives it great power over your life. It will then control you. You may never forget the infidelity, but time will diminish the pain and anger.

Ability to Recognize the Power of Thoughts for Healing

As Viktor Frankl, the psychiatrist and author of *Man's Search for Meaning*, has stated, "If one cannot change a situation that causes his suffering, he still can choose his attitude." This strong statement demonstrates that the way in which we see events can be a powerful coping skill. It becomes possible to survive by using thoughts for healing rather than prolonging pain.

You can use language and thought to calm yourself and put events into perspective. Catastrophizing and inventing worst-case scenarios are not the language of surviving. The spouse who thinks, "I will not survive the infidelity" will have more difficulty than the one who thinks, "The marriage will not survive, but I will."

In his book *Learned Optimism*, psychologist Martin Seligman explores the ins and outs of optimism and pessimism based on his twenty-five years of research and study. He tells us that optimists are less depressed because of the way they think about what has happened to them. Dr.

Seligman says that optimists "tend to believe defeat is just a temporary set-back and that its causes are confined to this one case." Pessimism may be deeply entrenched in the way an individual views the world, but Dr. Seligman goes on to say that this can be changed "by learning a new set of cognitive skills."

Survivors will not allow pessimistic thoughts to create a lifelong disaster for themselves. After dealing with the crisis of hearing about infidelity, the optimist is able to say to himself, "We need to find out why there was an affair and work to strengthen our marriage." Even if his wife decides to leave him for another man, the optimist, although sad, is still able to maintain his hope for the future.

Ability to Find Meaning in the Experience

Viktor Frankl speaks of this phenomenon from his own experience and observation in the Nazi concentration camps. He describes how inmates, who were undergoing one of the worst personal and group experiences known to humanity, were able to survive by looking for ways to find meaning in their suffering. "Fundamentally, therefore," he writes, "any man can, even under such circumstances, decide what shall become of him—mentally and spiritually. He may retain his human dignity even in a concentration camp."

Dr. Frankl saw that some inmates found meaning in their lives by not allowing the suffering to stop them from helping each other. Others found meaning in survival, so that they could live to bear witness to the Nazi atrocities. Others gave meaning to their lives and suffering by maintaining faith in God even through one of the worst horrors in history.

James Brady, former press secretary to President Ronald Reagan, sustained serious and crippling wounds when he was shot in a presidential assassination attempt. In the aftermath of this tragedy, Mr. Brady and his wife, Sarah, have found meaning in their work to increase the public's awareness of the danger of easy access to handguns. They have advocated the passage of what has become known as the Brady Bill, which makes access to guns more difficult.

We have all heard stories about parents whose children have been victims of senseless tragedies and who find meaning by helping others in similar circumstances. Organizations formed by parents whose children were killed by drunken drivers or were kidnapped are examples of using anger and pain as a way to find meaning in tragedy.

During the Republican and Democratic Conventions in 1992, the American public saw and heard two women whose lives had been deeply affected by AIDS. Mary Fisher and Elizabeth Glaser were trying to find meaning in their tragedy. They described the impact of AIDS on their lives in hopes of gathering support and encouraging political action to defeat this dreaded disease. Many advocacy groups and self-help groups have emerged to help people find meaning in their suffering.

Peggy Vaughn, author of *The Monogamy Myth*, has herself become a noted lecturer on infidelity after she and her husband worked through his infidelity. Not everyone starts advocacy organizations or lectures after surviving a pivotal experience in their lives, but most people are deeply influenced by such an experience.

• • •

As you begin the process of healing from the impact of infidelity on your life, we hope the skills and information you have gained from this book will help on your journey. We believe that, ultimately, you will transcend this experience, become stronger, and renew your faith in yourself and your ability to survive.

Love and Infidelity Quiz

Questions: Answer True or False

1. The idea of a marriage contract developed during the Middle Ages to protect men.

2. A woman's affair is a greater threat to a marriage than a man's.

3. There is a growing trend on the part of men to confess their affairs to their wives.

4. There is a rise in the number of women telling their husbands about their affairs.

5. Spouses are more likely to be faithful if they make an agreement to be faithful.

6. More men than women seek treatment for sexual addiction.

7. Someone who starts having affairs at an early age will most likely continue this behavior throughout the marriage.

8. The major reason people have affairs is to improve their sex lives.

9. Infrequent sexual contact between spouses indicates an unhappy marriage.

10. Husbands are less tolerant of their wives' having affairs than wives are of husbands' affairs.

11. Adultery laws are still on the books and enforced in some states.

12. Do-it-yourself erotic films are a safe way to spice up a couple's sex life with none of the dangers of an affair.

Answers to Quiz

1. False. The marriage contract predates the Middle Ages. The earliest one known dates back to 128 A.D. and was found with the Dead Sea Scrolls. The *Ketubah*, as it was called, was written in Aramaic and designed to protect a wife financially in case of divorce or widowhood.

2. True. A study by sociologist Annette Lawson showed his affair will be forgiven, while hers is likely to "threaten the marriage."

3. True. In her study on infidelity, Annette Lawson found that before 1965, only 47 percent of the husbands told their wives about their affairs, while in 1975, a total of 78 percent of the husbands told.

4. False. The reverse is true for women. There is a decline in the number of women confessing their infidelities to their husbands.

5. True. Lawson's studies have shown that there is more fidelity in marriage in which couples discuss their expectations.

6. True. Eighty percent of those who seek treatment for sexual addiction are men.

7. True. According to Lawson's studies, the earlier someone starts, "the more he/she will have" affairs.

8. False. People have affairs for many reasons. Studies show that sometimes sex is better in the affair, but most of the time it is not.

9. False. Studies show little or no relationship between frequency of sex and marital satisfaction.

10. True. Sociologists Philip Blumstein and Pepper Schwartz found a high correlation between the breakup of the marriage and telling their husbands about their infidelities.

11. True. In July 1990, after pleading guilty to adultery charges placed by her estranged husband, a Wisconsin homemaker was required to complete forty hours of community service and attend parenting classes. She could have received a jail sentence of up to two years and a $10,000 fine.

12. True. Many psychologists agree. A *Time* magazine article (October 29, 1990) reported that more and more couples are participating in homemade erotica, usually initiated by the husband.

References

Ansbacher, H.L., and Rowena Ansbacher eds. *The Individual Psychology of Alfred Adler*. New York: Basic Books, 1956.

Atwater, Lynn. *The Extramarital Connection*. New York: Irvington Publications, 1982.

Barbach, Lonnie. *For Each Other*. New York: New American Library, 1982.

Beck, Aaron T. *Cognitive Therapy and Emotional Disorders*. New York: New American Library, 1979.

Beck, Aaron T., John A Rush, Brian F. Shaw and Gary Emery. *Cognitive Therapy of Depression*. New York: Guilford Press, 1979.

Beck, Aaron T. *Love Is Never Enough*. New York: Harper and Row, 1988.

Bloomfield, Harold H., and Leonard Felder. *The Achilles Syndrome*. New York: Random House, 1985.

Bloomfield, Harold H., with Natasha Josefowitz. *Love Secrets For a Lasting Relationship*. New York: Bantam, 1992.

Blumstein, Phillip, and Pepper Schwartz. *American Couples*. New York: Pocket Books, 1985.

Botwin, Carol. *Men Who Can't Be Faithful*. New York: Warner Books, 1989.

Bowen, Murray. *Family Therapy In Clinical Practice*. New York: Jason Aaronson, 1978.

Brammer, L. et al. "Intervention Strategies for Coping with Transitions." *The Counseling Psychologist*. 9(2), 1981, 19-36.

Brody, Jane E. "Crying—It's Perfectly Normal for Women and Men." *The Democrat Press*. February 22, 1984.

Brown, Emily. *Patterns of Infidelity and Their Treatment*. New York: Brunner/Mazel, 1991.

Burns, David. *Intimate Connections*. New York: William Morrow and Company, 1985.

Burns, David. *Feeling Good*. New York: William Morrow and Company, 1989.

Burns, David. *The Feeling Good Handbook*. New York: William Morrow and Company, 1989.

Buscaglia, Leo. *Living, Loving and Learning*. Thorofare, New Jersey: Slack, Inc. 1982.

Carlson, Margaret. "Now Say It Like You Mean It." *Time*. September 14, 1998, 44.

Carnes, Patrick. *Out of the Shadows*. Center City, Minneapolis: Hazelden, 1992.

Chance, Susan. *Stronger Than Death: When Suicide Touches Your Life*. New York: W.W. Norton and Company, 1992.

Clanton, Gordon and Lynn Smith eds. *Jealousy*. Englewood Cliffs, New Jersey: Prentice-Hall, 1977.

Cochran, S.D., and V.M. Mays. "Sex, Lies, and HIV." *New England Journal of Medicine*, 322, 1990, 774-775.

Davis, Martha, Elizabeth Eshelman, and Matthew McKay. *The Relaxation and Stress Reduction Workbook*. Richmond, CA: New Harbinger Publications, 1980.

Daw, Jennifer. "Breaking the Seventh Commandment: Breaking the Law and Breaking the Trust." *Family Therapy News*, 29 (2), April/May 19998, 16-24.

Edwards, Maria. *The Challenge of Being Single*. New York: Signet, 1974.

Elliott, Timothy. "Counseling Adults from Schlossberg's Adaptation Model." *American Mental Health Counselors Association Journal*. 7(3), July 1985.

Ellis, Albert. *Growth Through Reason*. Palo Alto, CA: Science and Behavior Books, 1971.

Ellis, Albert. *A New Guide To Rational Living*. North Hollywood, CA: Wilshire Books, 1975.

Emery, Gary. *Getting Undepressed*. New York: Simon & Schuster 1988.

Ford, Charles V. *Lies, Lies, Lies*. Washington, D.C.: American Psychiatric Press Inc., 1996.

Frankl, Viktor E. *Man's Search For Meaning*. New York: Washington Square Press, 1963.

Glass, Shirley. "After Infidelity—Getting Beyond Betrayal." *Psychology Today*, August 1998.

Glass, Shirley, and Thomas L. Wright. "Restructuring Marriages after Extramarital Involvement." Presentation at American Association for Marriage and Family Therapy Conference, Washington, D.C., October 1990.

Glass, Shirley, and Thomas L. Wright. "Restructuring Marriages after The Trauma of Infidelity." In Kim Halford and Howard J. Markham, eds. *Clinical Handbook of Marriage and Couples Intervention*. New York: John Wiley & Sons, 1996, 471-507.

Haley, Jay. *Problem-Solving Therapy: New Strategies For Effective Family Therapy*. San Francisco: Jossey-Bass, 1976.

Harris, Gloria G., ed. *The Group Treatment of Human Problems*. New York: Grune & Stratton, 1977.

Heyn, Dalma. *The Erotic Silence of the American Wife*. New York: Turtle Bay, 1992.

Hollander, Dory. *101 Lies Men Tell Women*. New York, HarperCollins, 1995.

Holmes, Thomas H., and R. Rahe. "The Social Readjustment Rating Scale." *Journal of Psychosomatic Research*, II, 1967, 213-218.

Horsburgh, C. Robert, Jr., et al. "Duration of Human Immunodeficiency Virus Infection Before Detection of Antibody. *Lancet*, 1989, 637-639.

Hyde, Margaret O. and Elizabeth Forsyth. *Aids: What Does It Mean To You?* New York: Walker and Co., 1987.

Imber-Black, Evan, Janine Roberts, and Richard Whiting, eds. *Rituals in Families and Family Therapy*. New York: W.W. Norton and Company, 1988.

Jacobson, Neil, and Gayla Margolin, eds. *Marital Therapy*. New York: Brunner/Mazel, 1979.

Kaslow, Florence. "Attractions and Affairs: Fabulous and Fatal." Paper presented at the 1992 AAMFT Conference, October 15-18, Miami, Florida.

Kubler-Ross, Elizabeth. *On Death And Dying*. New York: Macmillan, 1969.

Kushner, Harold. *When Bad Things Happen To Good People*. New York: Avon, 1981.

Landers, Ann. Cited in *Time*, January 28, 1985, 76.

Langone, John. *Aids: The Facts*. Boston: Little, Brown, and Company, 1988.

Lasswell, Marcia, and Norman Lobsenz. "How to Handle Sexual Jealousy." *McCalls*, July 1977, 86-89.

Lauer, Robert and Jeanette. "Marriages Made to Last." *Psychology Today*, June 1985, 22-26.

Lawson, Annette. *Adultery*. New York: Basic Books, 1988.

Lerner, Harriet. *The Dance of Anger*. New York: Harper and Row, 1985.

Levinson, Daniel. *The Seasons of a Man's Life*. New York: Alfred A. Knopf, 1978.

Lusterman, Don-David. *Infidelity: A Survival Guide*. Oakland, CA: New Harbinger Publications, 1998.

Lusterman, Don-David. "Marriage at the Turning Point." *Networker*, May/June 1989, 44-51.

Madanes, Chloe. *Strategic Family Therapy*. San Francisco: Jossey-Bass, 1981.

——. *Behind The One-Way Mirror*. San Francisco: Jossey-Bass, 1988.

McGoldrick, Monica, and Randy Gerson. *Genograms in Family Assessment*. New York: W.W. Norton and Company, 1985.

McKay, Matthew, and Patrick Fanning. *Self-Esteem*. Richmond, CA: New Harbinger Publications, 1987.

Michaelis, David. "In the Shadow of the Patriarch." *Vanity Fair*, August 1998.

Miller, Sherod, David Wackman, Elam Nunnally, and Carol Saline. "Connecting in Bed." *San Diego Woman*, October 1992, 12-14.

Osborn, Susan M., and Gloria G. Harris. *Assertive Training For Women*. Springfield, IL.: Charles C. Thomas, 1975.

Parkes, Colin, and Robert Weiss. *Recovery From Bereavement*. New York: Basic Books, 1983.

Peck, M. Scott. *The Road Less Traveled*. New York: Simon & Schuster, 1978.

Pittman, Frank. *Private Lies*. New York: W.W. Norton, 1989.

Rabin, David and Pauline. *To Provide A Safe Passage: The Humanistic Aspects Of Science*. New York: Philosophical Library, 1985.

Reinisch, June. *The Kinsey Institute's New Report On Sex*. New York: St. Martin's Press, 1990.

Rubenstein, Carin, and Phillip Shaver. *In Search Of Intimacy*. New York: Delacorte, 1974.

Sager, Clifford. *Marriage Contracts and Couples Therapy*. New York: Brunner/Mazel, 1976.

Satir, Virginia. *Peoplemaking*. Palo Alto, CA: Science and Behavior Books, 1964.

Scarff, Maggie. *Intimate Partners*. New York: Random House, 1987.

Schlossberg, Nancy. "A Model for Analyzing Human Adaptation to Transitions." *Counseling Psychologist*, 9(2), 1981, 2-18.

——. *Counseling Adults In Transition*. New York: Springer, 1984.

Schneider, Jennifer. *Back From Betrayal*. New York: Ballantine Books, 1990.

Seligman, Martin E.P. *Learned Optimism*. New York: Pocket Books, 1986.

Shapiro, Allison. "Fantasy Affairs or Dangerous Liaisons?: Relations in the Cyberworld." *Family Therapy News*, February 1997, 12-13.

Sherman, Robert, and Norman Fredman. *Handbook of Structured Techniques In Marriage And Family Therapy*. New York: Brunner/Mazel, 1986.

Shulman, Bernard. *Contributions To Individual Psychology*. Chicago: Adler Institute, 1973.

Spring, Janis Abrahms. *After the Affair*. New York: HarperCollins, 1996.

Starr, Kenneth. *The Starr Report: A Report to Congress by the Independent Counsel on the President*. September 11, 1998.

Steinem, Gloria. *Revolution From Within: A Book Of Self-Esteem*. Boston: Little, Brown, and Company, 1992.

Sternberg, Robert. *The Triangle Of Love: Intimacy, Passion, And Commitment*. New York: Basic Books, 1988.

Stuart, Richard B. *Helping Couples Change*. New York: Guilford Press, 1980.

Tavris, Carol. *Anger: The Misunderstood Emotion*. New York: Touchstone/Simon & Schuster, 1982.

Trotter, Robert J. "The Three Faces of Love." *Psychology Today*, September 1986, 47-54.

Vaughn, Peggy. *The Monogamy Myth*. New York: Newmarket Press, 1989.

Viorst, Judith. "Confessions of a Jealous Wife." In Gordon Clanton and Lynn Smith, eds. *Jealousy*. Englewood Cliffs, New Jersey: Prentice-Hall, 1977.

———. *Necessary Losses*. New York: Ballantine Books, 1986.

Weiss, Robert. *Marital Separation*. New York: Basic Books, 1975.

———. *Going It Alone*. New York: Basic Books, 1979.

Weitzman, Lenore. *The Divorce Revolution: The Unsuspected Social and Economic Consequences For Women And Children In America*. New York: The Free Press, 1985.

Index

Emotional upsets, cognitive
approach to coping with, 85
Empathy in resolving issues of
infidelity, 48
Empty love, 122
Erotic films, 205, 206
Events
ability to see complexity of,
198
ability to view, in time frame,
199
negative interpretation of,
87–88
Everly, George, 101
Exit affair, 54–55
Expectations
in post-affair marriage, 148–49
unfulfilled, as reason for affairs,
39–42
Experience, ability to find
meaning in, 202–3
Extramarital sex, role in
dissolution of many
marriages, 13

F
Family
death in, as life transition, 37
interactions in, and self-esteem,
189–90
loyalties in, as problem in
divorce, 169
Family affair, 52–53
Family history of extramarital
affairs, 34–35
Farrow, Mia, 53
Fears
of conflict, 107
of creating worse
problems, 107
of rejection, 107

role of, in keeping you in
marriage, 121
of "what if," 107
Feelings
ability to withstand
uncomfortable, 196–97
impact of thinking on,
85–93
Films, erotic, 205, 206
Fisher, Mary, 203
Flings, 26–28, 117
sexually transmitted diseases in,
25–26
Ford, Charles, 58
Forgiving, 132, 145–46
Fortune telling, 89–90
Frankl, Viktor, 201, 202
Future, negative expectations
of, 88

G
Gender differences
in deception, 60–62
and repairing relationships,
133–35
Genital warts, 126
Glaser, Elizabeth, 203
Glass, Shirley, 49, 59, 69,
133–34, 136
Grief and loss, 79–82
Guilt in revealing past affair, 67

H
Hart, Gary, 24
Healing, ability to recognize
power of thoughts for, 201–2
Help, ability to ask for, 200–201
Helplessness, sense of, 53–54
Hepburn, Katharine, 30
Herpes, 126
Heyn, Dalma, 62

About the Authors

Rona Subotnik is a licensed Marriage and Family Counselor and is a Clinical Member of the American Association of Marriage and Family Therapists.

She received her M.A. in counseling from Trinity College in Washington, D.C. For eight years, she worked at A Woman's Place, an innovative counseling center, which is a program of the Commission for Women of the Montgomery County, Maryland government. There, she did individual therapy and designed and led numerous workshops and counseling groups for women, one of which was called "Surviving Infidelity."

Mrs. Subotnik also taught in the Graduate Studies Department of Trinity College and the Women's Studies Program at Mt. Vernon College in Washington, D.C.

She is married, has three grown children, and lives with her husband, Norman, in La Jolla, California. She is in private practice in San Diego, California.

Gloria G. Harris, Ph.D. received her doctorate in clinical psychology from the University of Washington. She has co-authored *Assertive Training for Women* and edited *The Group Treatment of Human Problems*. Her faculty appointments have included the University of Washington Medical School, American University, and San Diego State University.

Dr. Harris has served as a member of the Board of Directors of the San Diego Psychological Association, the San Diego County Commission on Children and Youth, and the San Diego County Mental Health Advisory Board. She is currently the Chair of the San Diego County Commission on the Status of Women. She is married, has two grown children, and lives with her husband, Jay, in La Jolla, California. She is in private practice in San Diego, California.